Manchester
in the Victorian Age

1   Market Street, Manchester, around 1890 *overleaf*

Gary S. Messinger

MANCHESTER
IN THE
VICTORIAN AGE
The half-known city

'Rightly understood,
Manchester is as great a
human exploit as Athens.'
Benjamin Disraeli,
Coningsby (1844)

MANCHESTER
UNIVERSITY PRESS

Copyright © Gary S. Messinger 1985
Published by Manchester University Press
Oxford Road, Manchester M13 9PL, UK
and 51 Washington Street, Dover,
New Hampshire 03820, USA

British Library cataloguing in publication data
Messinger, Gary S.
    Manchester in the Victorian age : the half-known city.
    1. Manchester (Greater Manchester)—History
    I. Title
    942.7'33081   DA690.M4

Library of Congress cataloging in publication data
Messinger, Gary S., 1943–
    Manchester in the Victorian age.
    ¯Bibliography: p. 199
    Includes index.
    1. Manchester (Greater Manchester)   I. Title.
DA690.M4M57   1985   942.7'33081   85-5141
ISBN 0-7190-1814-5 *cased*
ISBN 0-7190-1843-9 *paper*

Printed in Great Britain
at the Alden Press, Oxford

Contents

II. THE INDUSTRIAL METROPOLIS

List of Illustrations

The publishers acknowledge their gratitude to the following for
permission to reproduce the illustrations. Mr Gamble, 32. *The
Guardian* and Denis Thorpe, 33. Chris Makepeace, 1, 3, 4, 5, 31.
Manchester City Art Gallery, 18, 25, 26. Manchester Public
Libraries, 6, 10, 13, 17, 19, 21, 22, 29, 30. National Portrait Gallery,
11, 12, 14. John Rylands Library, 15. Portico Library, 16, 28.
Manchester Lit & Phil, 20, 23, 27. Public Relations Office,
Manchester Town Hall, 24. Eddie Cass, 8 Quarry Bank Mill, 9.

TO JAVAID SADIQ
of Manchester and Lahore
who introduced me to
the British Commonwealth of Nations

Acknowledgements

This work would not have been possible without the assistance and advice of many individuals and institutions. While I was a graduate student at Harvard University, the late David Owen inspired my interest in British history. After his death, work continued under H. J. Hanham, then of Harvard, now Dean of Humanities at Massachusetts Institute of Technology, who encouraged my interest in Manchester and directed my doctoral thesis on the imagery of the city in the early nineteenth century. Over the years, during research trips to Manchester, I have benefited greatly from the kindness and wise criticisms of many local residents, particularly W. H. Chaloner, R. C. Richardson, Arthur Rose, and Robert Walmsley. Like numerous other researchers, I have enjoyed extensive assistance from the staff of the Christie Library at the University of Manchester and the staff of the Local History Section at Manchester Central Reference Library, particularly Christopher Makepeace and Alan Barlow. Hilda Lofthouse provided frequent help during visits to Chetham's Library. The skill and good humor of Sidney Horrocks and others on the staff of the Committee for a Lancashire Bibliography greatly aided the search for documents. At Manchester University Press, Ray Offord, Juanita Griffiths, and other members of the staff provided excellent counsel throughout the editorial process. For unfailing support, penetrating criticisms, and continuing encouragement, I am deeply grateful to my parents, Jack and Florine Messinger, my sister, Linda, and my wife, Cleo. My thanks to one other individual are recorded in the dedication. Any deficiencies this work may contain are my responsibility, not those of the above named persons and organisations.

Introduction

This work is a historical survey of Manchester during the years when it was the most important industrial city in the world. The book makes available under one cover the basic information on Manchester in the nineteenth century: its role as the cradle of the industrial revolution, the site of the Peterloo riot of 1819, the subject of novels by Charles Dickens, Benjamin Disraeli and Elizabeth Gaskell, the headquarters of the Anti-Corn Law League and the free trade movement, the classroom of the Manchester school of economics, the northern capital of England, and the home of the Hallé concerts and the *Manchester Guardian*. But the book differs from other surveys in print in that it concentrates on Victorian Manchester, 1837-1901, rather than the earlier years of industrialisation. Pre-Victorian Manchester is covered, including a number of developments which have not received great attention elsewhere, such as Manchester's contributions to the public health movement and the study of social statistics in the 1830s. But these subjects are included chiefly to help the reader see the city's foundations, and the largest amount of space is reserved for later events in Manchester's history which are less widely understood although they were of equally national and international importance: the Art Treasures Exhibition of 1857, the first public library in the realm, leadership in the national movement for university expansion, construction of Manchester's new town hall, the symbolic importance of the Manchester Ship Canal, the growing influence of the *Manchester Guardian,* Manchester's role as a centre of Irish nationalism, the interest the city held for members of the utopian crafts movement in the late nineteenth century, the city's role in the women's suffrage movement, the emergence among Manchester residents of a distinct type of urban personality, and the great attention paid to the city by social and economic and political theorists throughout the world.

The book focuses upon Manchester's contributions to national life. It also pays attention to the thoughts and feelings of contemporaries. The Victorians lived through one of the great ages of urban growth in world history. In some ways they understood this fact quite well; in other ways they understood it not at all. We learn more about them and about ourselves if we recall the sense of mystery which residents of Manchester and other nineteenth century cities so frequently expressed.

The book concludes with a brief epilogue noting some of the key events in the history of twentieth century Manchester and assessing the permanent significance of Manchester's experience. The focus remains throughout, however, on the mid and late nineteenth century. Manchester is essentially a Victorian city. Whoever wishes to understand it, even today, must review that earlier era.

PART I

The industrial city

CHAPTER 1

The first industrial city

In 1814, in a lengthy poem entitled *The Excursion,* William Wordsworth gave his impressions of the new manufacturing districts of northern England. In awe the poet wrote:

Meanwhile, at social Industry's command,
How quick, how vast an increase! From the germ
Of some poor hamlet, rapidly produced
Here a huge town, continuous and compact,
Hiding the face of earth for leagues – and there,
Where not a habitation stood before,
Abodes of men irregularly massed
Like trees in forests, – spread through spacious tracts,
O'er which the smoke of unremitting fires
Hangs permanent, and plentiful as wreaths
Of vapour glittering in the morning sun. [Book VIII]

To the 'huge town' mentioned in these lines Wordsworth gave no name. For him it could easily have been any one of a hundred centres of industry that had suddenly appeared in the area men and women were beginning to call 'the manufacturing regions'. Even as his lines were being published, however, one element in his composite was already beginning to impress the poet's contemporaries as the embodiment of all the changes he described. To ask why this element, Manchester, should have attracted so much attention is to raise a question of fundamental importance for the history of the modern world.

From Roman Fort to Boom Town. Manchester lies at the middle of the great Lancashire plain, an area which resembles a vast amphitheatre. To the west the plain extends in a continuous, flat expanse as far as the Irish Sea. To the south it merges into the low, hilly countryside of Cheshire and Derbyshire. To the north and east the landscape rises in a series of valleys and

2   Peter Street in the 1820's, with St Peter's Church among the mill chimneys

ever higher mountain slopes near the borders of Cumberland, Westmoreland, and Yorkshire. Out of this crescent-shaped area numerous brooks pour southward and westward into three meandering rivers: the Irwell, which runs roughly north to south; the Irk, which runs east to west; and the Medlock, which runs roughly parallel to the Irk some two miles below it. All three streams eventually join the Mersey and reach the sea at Liverpool. But to the north-east of Liverpool the three rivers converge. Here the land remains relatively low – and is interrupted by a number of bluffs along the river banks.

For prehistoric tribesmen this area provided defence and shelter. Later, in the second century A.D., the Romans constructed a fort near the junction of the Irwell and the Medlock. They called their creation Mancunium (hence the modern term 'Mancunians' to describe Manchester residents) and made it one of the centres of the communications network for the north-west region; at least six and perhaps seven Roman roads converge there. Records do not disclose whether the Saxons continued to maintain the site after the Romans withdrew in the late fourth or early fifth century. By Norman times, however, Manchester possessed a large, well built castle from which a lord of the manor administered the area. The Church had designated the town as the headquarters of one of the largest parishes in the realm, and efforts were under way to give Manchester an imposing cathedral. In addition, the groundwork was being laid for the development which was to be the greatest expansive force of all, the growth of the textile industry.

As early as 1282, the date of the first written reference on the subject, Manchester already possessed an appreciable trade in textiles, probably linen and wool. By the time of the reign of Henry VIII, cloth manufacture had become so vital in the area that the privilege of sanctuary was removed from the town in order to protect the trade from rogues and vagabonds who disrupted the drying of wool and the spreading of linen yarn in open, sunlit fields. By the end of the sixteenth century the town had begun to expand into the production of other fabrics. Usually called 'Manchester cottons', 'cotton wool', and 'fustians', these cloths were made from various combinations of wool, linen, flax and cotton imported from the Near East. It was cotton, however, which soon came to have the greatest importance for the town's economic development, probably because moist climate and water with a high content of limestone made the area more suitable for weaving this fibre than other parts of England. So rapidly did the cotton manufacture expand that, by 1724, Daniel Defoe described Manchester as 'the greatest mere village in England'. The town to which Defoe referred was also growing in political importance. It was a major stronghold of the Puritans during the civil wars of the seventeenth century, and was later used as headquarters of the Stuart cause during the Jacobite uprisings of 1715 and 1745.

In these years the cotton industry was still unmechanised and was spread in domestic workshops throughout Lancashire. Manchester itself served as a centre for the processes by which the fabric was finished and as a market place from which the famous 'Manchester packmen' transported their goods on strings of horses led along the roads to surrounding towns, to the port at Liverpool, or to the eastern counties by way of the hazardous, robber-infested bridle paths of the Pennines. Around 1750 economic centrality entered a new stage. To the south, the growing port of Liverpool provided the stimulus of overseas trade. With the gradual dredging of the Irwell, it became possible by 1750 for boats of sixty tons to ply between Manchester and the coast. Construction of turnpikes allowed for increased use of waggons and carts. The Bridgewater Canal, opened in 1761, was the first of a succession of similar wonders of engineering which began to link the area in a vast economic net. Coaching services also improved, the 'Flying Coach' from Manchester to London requiring four and a half days' journey in 1754 but only thirty hours by the end of the century.

Meanwhile, on countless streams in the hinterland, mills were being started in line with the first stages of automation of the cotton industry, a movement made possible by the extraordinary genius of Lancashire inventors, such as Richard Arkwright of Preston, inventor of the water-powered spinning frame, and Samuel Crompton of Bolton, inventor of the 'mule', which made production of fine thread possible.

Inventors and mills soon converged on the town, as gradual improvement of steam power ended dependence on locating near a stream and allowed mill owners to take advantage of central supporting services. The first steam-powered cotton mill was set up in Manchester in the 1780s; by 1794 there were three; soon there were many more. Subsidiary functions multiplied: ropemaking, metalworking, glass making, bleaching and dyeing; banks for providing capital and accounting services; construction to take up the task of building the houses needed for the growing number of factory workers; clothing makers; food marketers; keepers of public houses; and shopkeepers of every description.

The whole process became cumulative, much like the later 'boom towns' of Australia, Alaska or the American west. Manchester had roots that no boom town ever had, and it was by no means totally lawless. Nevertheless, in the years before 1850 Lancashire was faced with the task of absorbing more migrants than either Canada or Australia. Manchester welcomed all comers, promising the chance of steady wages and even riches in exchange for the raw life one was forced to lead there. The town was unable to provide the services needed to keep pace with expansion, but even this fact was of paradoxical advantage. The alternative, judging from other towns, was probably an oligarchical municipal corporation that would have channelled Manchester's growth in line with its own narrow interests. Instead, Manchester was an extraordinarily open town which took full advantage of its position between a geographic frontier to the north and an economic frontier to the south. It became a kind of Eldorado. From the farms, villages and towns of neighbouring areas, successive waves of English labourers migrated towards it. From across the sea came the poor of Ireland. From the north came Scotsmen fleeing the harsh life of the Highlands and the slums of Edinburgh and Glasgow. And from the Continent more settlers arrived: some fleeing religious persecutions, others fleeing civil strife, such as Greeks during the revolution of 1821 and Italians during the wars leading to national unification in the 1840s; others, under clandestine conditions, either offering to sell or hoping to steal the secrets of new industrial techniques; still others, particularly the large number of Germans from Hanseatic cities, attracted by the chance of high monetary return for their business skills. Population increased at an astonishing rate. In the 1780s Manchester contained some 40,000 inhabitants; in 1801, the year of the first national census, the figure had reached more than 70,000. If the adjacent suburb of Salford was included, then Manchester, with over 84,000 inhabitants, was by 1801 the second most populous town of Great Britain. Only London – 'the Metropolis' – was larger.

A portent. Growth on this scale posed fundamental problems of perception. Contemporaries would have known that other cities, at other times in history, had been more important than Manchester in terms of cultural life or size or total population; and that other cities had at least equalled it as centres where science or handicrafts or vast accumulations of organised labour led to rapid technological development. Educated Englishmen could have cited ancient Athens and Rome as more impressive than Manchester on all these counts. Even easier were comparisons with the cities of the Low Countries, with their extensive trade and textile industries. And there was always the example of London. Nevertheless, contemporaries could find no complete precedent for Manchester.

To the present-day historian the reasons for this perplexity are clear. A modern observer can see that Manchester was the first predominantly industrial city in the history of the world. No other town had ever been so much given over to the demands of the factory system. And in no other town had the techniques of production by steam-powered machinery ever been applied so extensively. Contemporaries, of course, could not view matters in this perspective. But they did sense that Manchester's growth posed a challenge to the understanding which demanded resolution.

One response was to see the changes which had come over Manchester simply as an extension of traditional features. Cockfighting, bear baiting, streets dominated by ancient half-timbered houses, rushbearing ceremonies held in a medieval Collegiate Church, a system of local government dating back to William the Conqueror – these and similar features of town life provided ample evidence, even as late as 1800, that all the changes in Manchester might simply lead to what one twentieth century analyst of cities in Asia and Africa, Gideon Sjoberg, has termed 'the pre-industrial city'. This helps to explain the tardiness of many citizens of Manchester in proposing methods to deal with rapid change.

A growing number of contemporaries did realise, however,

that certain details could not be explained by eighteenth century categories. One puzzling element was Manchester's rapid sprawl. About 1772, wrote a member of Manchester's recently established club of gentleman scientists, the Literary and Philosophical Society, 'The town extended on every side, and such was the influx of inhabitants, that, though a great number of houses were built, they were occupied even before they were finished.' By the 1820s the writer of an early town guidebook recollected, 'During the last fifty years, perhaps no town in the United Kingdom has made such rapid improvements as Manchester. Every year has witnessed an increase of buildings, churches, chapels, places of amusement, and an immensity of streets have started into existence with a rapidity which has constantly afforded matter for astonishment in the minds of occasional visitors.'

Hills were flattened, trees cut down, farms and fields replaced by town squares and factory buildings. Increasingly, observers sensed, objects of orientation in the Manchester area were not natural, but were artifacts of the town. Contemplating the prospect of the town from afar, a guidebook writer of 1813 warned visitors, 'The beauties consist rather in objects of art than of nature; for, whenever a country becomes populous, nature is always compelled to give way to the convenience or the caprice of man.' The entire area, said the same observer, was 'nearly barren of antiquities, the whole being a structure of yesterday, and arising out of the commercial prosperity of Great Britain. We have here no Arcadia, in which to place shepherds with their pipes; for the country is to be looked upon as completely a manufacturing, and not as a pastoral.'

Also vividly noted by contemporaries was the increased inte gration of urban functions which the factory system was producing. Manchester was compared to a delicate mechanism, a break in one part drastically affecting all other parts. In 1801, after visiting a cotton mill, one observer remarked that its principles guided the whole town. Truly to understand the factory, he said, one had to 'conceive a population of seventy and eighty thousand people, for the most part busily employed in the various branches of useful manufacture, . . . the whole mighty wheel moved, invigorated, and accelerated by a capital of ten millions of money' (Richard Warner). Later writers pressed the concept

3   Bancks & Co's 'Plan of Manchester with the most recent improvements' 1828

Plan of
MANCHESTER
with the most recent Improvements.
1828

References

of integration even further. At first they merely stressed that Manchester was the economic leader of the Lancashire region, and that surrounding factory towns like Oldham, Rochdale and Stockport formed the 'vassal country' (Kinder Wood, 1813) over which it ruled. By the early 1820s, however, the notion of integration had become so common that one writer could see worldwide implications in the fact that the life of 'circumjacent towns and villages' had 'progressively verged towards Manchester'. Like a 'large circuitous and overwhelming vortex', the town had 'engulphed all the art, science, industry, activity and wealth, of a great part of this populous and powerful empire', and for this reason had become more important to Britain's international economic position than any other town of the realm (James Butterworth, 1823).

With increased integration of function came a change of mood, the sheer excitement of seeing the new power of science and technology. Thus, as early as 1781, Matthew Boulton wrote to James Watt, 'The people in Manchester are all steam-mill mad.' Added to such feelings was an almost total transformation of the patterns in which people received their impressions of town life. In 1809 a pamphlet was issued for visitors to Manchester, entitled *Directions for Walking the Streets of Manchester and the Conduct of Carriages.* Of the town's main thoroughfare it remarked, '. . . in walking down Market-street-lane to the Exchange, it is likely that a person will be pushed all ways, at least twenty times, sometimes against the houses, others off the flags, notwithstanding his endeavour to walk regular; the fact is, without rule you are forced in and out, running against one another, to the annoyance of all, and the hindrance of those upon business; who being anxious to get forward, push along irregularly and increase the confusion.'

Urban impressions became more intensified as other towns began to develop in line with the patterns Manchester had already followed. Technologically and economically the cotton industry led the way in the development of the factory system. Then, as its techniques were taken up and adapted by the manufacturers of wool, iron, steel and other products, towns began to emerge all over Britain which either wholly or partially imitated Manchester. In 1826, when William Cobbett visited the developing town of Frome, in Somerset, he called it 'a sort

4   Market Street in the 1820's

of little Manchester'. 'A very small Manchester indeed,' he explained, 'but it has all the *flash* of a Manchester, and the innkeepers and their people look and behave like Manchester fellows.'

Compressed in Cobbett's remark was the assumption of a discernible trend of urban development. If one sensed this trend, contemporaries came to feel, one had a key to the future. It was perhaps inevitable that such a powerful analytic tool should be given mystical overtones. Thus Manchester became in the minds of many a portent. To approach it as one descended from the Pennines to the smoky Lancashire plain; to ride into it by the bumpy cobblestone roads from London or Liverpool; to walk its streets and to be bombarded by the symbolic impressions it gave off — all this was to experience a magical revelation that one had found the means to an understanding of Britain's development. Only gradually would observers be able to sort out the 'part for whole' fallacy to which this feeling could often lead. In the early years the excitement of discovery ruled over logical caution.

The optimists. The most common result was positive inspiration in the face of benevolent potential. As early as 1757, a then well known poem by John Dyer, entitled *The Fleece,* ex pressed this mood. The poet described the growing industrialisation of the cotton industry, stating, 'all is here in motion, all is life', and then continued:

> th' echoing hills repeat
> The stroke of ax and hammer; scaffolds rise,
> And growing edifices; heaps of stone,
> Beneath the chissel, beauteous shapes assume
> Of frize and column. Some, with even line,
> New streets are marking in the neighb'ring fields,
> And sacred domes of worship. Industry,
> Which dignifies the artist, lifts the swain,
> And the straw cottage to a palace turns,
> Over the work presides. . .
> So appear
> Th' increasing walls of busy Manchester,
> Sheffield, and Birmingham, whose redd'ning fields
> Rise and enlarge their suburbs. Lo, in throngs,
> For ev'ry realm, the careful factors meet,
> Whisp'ring each other. In long ranks and bales,
> Like war's bright files, beyond the sight extend.

By 1777 the mood of these lines had become focused on Manchester specifically. In that year a Manchester resident published a series of letters to a friend at Cambridge, in which he offered several doggerel 'Sketches of Manchester in Verse', denigrating pastoral imagery and exhorting readers to see that Manchester had its full share of beauties:

What are dreams upon Pindus, or drafts of its springs,
To the joy, solid joy, which the compting-house brings?

The poet described the River Irwell:

. . . behold! in this mirror of dull, muddy hue,
The full dwellings of Trade pictur'd out to the view.
How the lines of tall structures embrace either side.

Then the cotton manufacture:

Busy movements of wheels whizzing loud thro' the air;
Some at distance behind, in swift course to and fro,
Thro' the loom shoot the shuttle, like shafts from a bow.

Then the din of commerce:

From the full, varied scenes of mix'd tumult and noise,
Midst the car's frequent roar, and retailer's shrill cries,

And finally, after a long catalogue of other impressions, some thoughts on the sheer pleasure of association:

From cares disengag'd, as I rove thro' the streets,
Such as move the quick step of the crowds that one meets,
How the heart with kind warmth teems enlarg'd at the view,
While the eyes the gay scenes in due order pursue!

By the time of these lines, Manchester's version of the standard urban 'boosterism' was already well established. To men of this persuasion, Manchester seemed an incarnation of great creative forces, a proof of the beneficent effects of man's triumph over the forces of nature. The economic and industrial miracles which the town exhibited daily were a source of wonder, and grounds for boundless hope in the human future. As early as 1783 the author of the first Manchester guidebook could remark in his subtitle that his description of the town would include 'A Succinct History of its former original manufactories and their gradual advancement to the present state of perfection at which they are arrived'. And by 1823 an early historian of the cotton trade could declare: 'That the envelope of a small seed, of an insignificant appearance, should by undergoing various operations and processes, ultimately be the great means of raising this town, and even the empire itself, to the highest meridian of splendour, and of commerical glory, in the short space of about half a century, is wonderful indeed!' Such remarks were the beginning of a long tradition of urban optimism.

The pessimists.   In the midst of all this confidence, observers of different mood were expressing their attitude. 'Oh! What a dog hole is Manchester!' commented the future Viscount Torrington in 1792. As an upholder of the landed aristocracy, he was particularly well placed to see the problems of urbanisation which Manchester dramatised. 'I see the hearty husbandman suck'd into the gulph of sickly traffic; and whilst some towns swell into unnatural numbers, lost is the sturdy yeoman, and honest cottager!' Equally critical was Richard Holden, a solicitor from nearby Rotherham. Visiting Manchester in 1808, he remarked, 'The town is abominably filthy, the Steam Engines pestiferous, the Dyehouses noisesome and offensive, and the Water of the River as black as Ink or the Stygian Lake.'

In the same vein were the criticisms of the Poet Laureate, Robert Southey. In 1807 a mere visit to Manchester prompted him to attack the entire English manufacturing system. He compared Manchester's population to Helots and was reminded of 'the cities in Arabian romance, where all the inhabitants were enchanted; here Commerce is the queen witch, and I had no talisman strong enough to disenchant those who were daily drinking of the golden cup of her charms,' He concluded, 'A place more destitute of all interesting objects than Manchester it is not easy to conceive. In size and population it is the second city of the kingdom, containing above fourscore thousand inhabitants. Imagine this multitude crowded together in narrow streets, the houses all built of brick and blackened with smoke: frequent buildings among them as large as convents, without their antiquity, without their beauty, without their holiness, where you hear from within, as you pass along, the everlasting din of machinery; and where when the bell rings it is to call wretches to their work instead of their prayers . . .' As in the case of the urban 'boosters', these remarks signalled the beginning of a long tradition. Unable to find ground for optimism in the portent of Manchester, Southey was to be only one of many who watched and were afraid.

CHAPTER 2

The cotton industry and its world

The basis of Manchester's expansion was a small, shrublike plant of the genus *Gossypium,* cultivated in warm climates throughout the world because of the soft, white, downy fibre which appeared in buds when the seeds on the plant's branches broke open their brown hulls and entered fruition. The earliest records of cotton cultivation to make cloth were in India and Egypt. By the eighteenth century cotton was also important to the economies of China, Turkey and Asia Minor, each area cultivating its own variety. Indian fibre, for example, was generally short and brittle – partly because of soil and climate, partly because of inefficient agriculture. Egyptian cotton, on the other hand, had long, soft, strong fibres and was considered the best in the world. By the end of the eighteenth century cotton had also become an important crop in the southern United States. Here a number of varieties were cultivated, such as the brittle, short-fibred cotton of Mississippi and the long-fibred cotton grown in the sea islands of South Carolina.

Originally cotton was spun and woven by handicraft methods using sticks, spindles, spinning wheels and hand looms. But in western Europe, England in particular, the industrial revolution created a capacity to refine raw materials far in advance of the rest of the world, so that, by the late eighteenth century, India and Egypt were exporters of raw cotton to Britain. By 1820, however, the major source of supply had become the slave holding areas of the United States, which enjoyed competitive advantages because of favourable soil and climate, vast acreage, and a supply of cheap African labour able to work long hours in the sun and humidity. These advantages were compounded in 1793 when the American Eli Whitney developed a new kind of cotton gin which greatly speeded separation of the cotton bud from its hull.

The cotton manufacture. From Calcutta and Bombay, from Alexandria, from New Orleans, Mobile, Savannah and Charleston, from hundreds of other ports around the world, the cotton was shipped across the oceans. Originally the major part of it had been unloaded at London. By the late eighteenth century, as Manchester became the centre of manufacture, Liverpool was the major cotton port of England. Here the bales were unloaded and stored in great warehouses until they could be sold by private contract, at auction, or through brokers to 'dealers' from Manchester, who shipped their purchases north-east – in the late eighteenth century by waggon or barge, after the 1830s, ever more frequently by railway. Arriving in Manchester, the bales were again unloaded and then either stored in the dealer's sheds or warehouses to await sale, or carted direct to the warehouses of cotton manufacturers who had already purchased supplies from a dealer and wanted immediate delivery.

Arriving at the manufacturer's, the cotton was ready for processing. Seeds were removed. The cotton was washed and dried. It was then carded and made ready for spinning into yarn, after which the yarn would be woven into cloth and then 'finished' by various processes of bleaching, dyeing and printing. In the early years of the industrial revolution many of these steps were performed by the same manufacturer. As the nineteenth century progressed, each function became an elaborate speciality.

All the steps as far as spinning might be performed by one factory, which would then sell its product to a yarn agent, who passed the goods on to a weaving factory. The weaver took the process as far as producing 'grey cloth', which was then passed on – although with the help of another agent – to the finishers, who were in fact many different firms. Packing and shipping of finished cloth also became specialties in their own right.

The many cash transactions accompanying these arrangements were negotiated for the most part at a central gathering place in Manchester which came to be called the 'exchange'. The first Exchange building had been constructed in 1729. It was torn down in 1790, with replacement completed in 1806. Ever larger buildings were to follow throughout the nineteenth

5   Phillip's Mill, Ancoats, 1795

century.

The two great 'sections' of the cotton industry, as they came to be called, were 'yarn' and 'cloth'. Yarn encompassed not only the thicker, heavier varieties but also the finer counts, sometimes called 'threads'. The second category, cloth, also sometimes called cotton 'goods', encompassed an ever growing variety of fabrics. Some were imitations in cotton of fabrics that had been manufactured for centuries by the silk and woollen industries of eastern and southern England and continental Europe. Others were creations of the weavers of Manchester and Lancashire themselves. Still others were English copies of cloths known to the British from their overseas contracts with the unmechanised cloth production of India and the Far East. Baft, baize, bandana, bombazine, brocade, calico, cambric, canvas, chintz, corduroy, crepe, cretonne, denim, dhootie, dimity, drill, duck, flannelette, fustian, gauze, gingham, jacconet, jean, khaki, linen, long cloth, matting, moleskin, mull, muslin, nankeen, Oxford, rep, sarong, sateen, sheeting, shirting, ticking, twill, velveteen. Each of these fabrics had a history and a romance of its own. Each called for special skills on the part of the manufacturer and each could be the object of a life's work.

The cotton trade. Once it had become yarn or cloth, the cotton production of Manchester was ready to be sold and, in almost every case, shipped to another locality. If marketed domestically, in the 'home trade', it could reach a variety of destinations. Fine grades of yarn, for example, might be sold to dealers in Nottingham, where quality lace making had been a staple of the economy since the Middle Ages.

The various cloths also took their own routes. Canvas, for example, might be sent to the port cities of the realm for use by sail makers. More durable grades of satin might be purchased by dealers for resale to upholsterers and furniture makers. Shirting cloths, early in the nineteenth century, might be sold to individual shopkeepers in towns and cities throughout Britain where the cloths would be purchased by tailors, housewives, seamstresses and domestics, to make clothing for their families and employers. By the mid-nineteenth century huge quantities of cotton fabric were also being sold to the garment industry – centred in London, with major facilities in Northern Ireland as well – which had attracted the public into buying ready-made shirts, trousers, dresses, underclothing and other garments which had been sewn at home in previous decades.

Other cotton fabrics and their users included khaki cloth, purchased by the military for uniforms; 'lasting cloth', a stiff, hardy fabric used by shoemakers; brattice cloth, used for lining the sides of mine shafts; sponge cloth, used for cleaning machinery; and certain varieties of cotton fabric which were used to make lamp wicks and even billiard balls.

All the goods sold in the home trade were also marketed in the 'export trade'. In this sphere, before 1850, Manchester enjoyed huge competitive advantages. In industrial development it was several decades ahead of places such as Lyons, the Rhineland or the New England region of the United States where sophisticated cotton manufacture was to appear in the latter half of the nineteenth century. This meant, as well, that the whole world was Manchester's potential market – especially after the defeat of Napoleon in 1815, when the major trade routes of the world were controlled by British sea power. As early as 1785 Britain was already exporting over £1 million worth of cotton yarns and goods in a year. By 1816, the figure had jumped to £16 million, by 1851 to £31 million.

Even when France, Germany and the United States began in later decades to meet the needs of their own home markets, these countries still did not compete powerfully with Britain in sales of cotton products to other nations such as India and China. In the period 1899-1903, for example, Germany's total exports of yarns and cloth amounted to £13.7 million per annum. In the same period Britain's exports amounted to approximately £67 million annually. As late as 1900 all Massachusetts had fewer power-driven spindles than the single Lancashire town of Oldham.

The distribution of wealth. Taken together, the home trade and the export trade transformed Manchester into a very prosperous city. Large, well-built factories, increasingly opulent warehouses and a superabundance of banks were perhaps the most obvious signs of this wealth. One could see it, as well, in the growing number of literary, scientific and philanthropic institutions which became part of the city's life, such as the

Literary and Philosophical Society (founded 1781); the Portico Library and Club, and the Royal Manchester Institution for the pursuit of science (both founded in 1823); the Athenaeum (founded 1835); and the new journals such as the *Manchester Guardian* (founded 1821) and the *Manchester Courier* (founded 1825). For those sections of the population able to take advantage of such institutions, living conditions were often quite pleasant. Included in this group were the better paid factory operatives with highly marketable skills; foremen in factories and warehouses; better paid clerks from the city's business offices; members of the professions; most teachers and members of the clergy; shopkeepers who dealt with the middle and upper classes; and of course the successful merchants and manufacturers. For wealthier citizens in particular, life could be especially comfortable; from the 1830s onwards large suburban villas began to appear in property developments on the southern perimeter of the city.

One of the features most noted by outside observers, however, was the relatively small number of people who enjoyed living conditions of tolerable level. It was upon the vast mass of workers that visitors focused when they wanted to emphasise the character of social relations in Manchester. The favourite comparison was with Birmingham, where labour in such activities as ironworking was generally conducted in small workshops with one master in fairly close *rapport* with ten or twenty employees. In Manchester the cotton industry dictated a more impersonal system. A hundred or more operatives might find themselves in a huge room supervised by a few overseers, with the owner of the mill some distant presence. Even though mill owners and overseers often worked as hard as or harder than the men they drove, and even though many factory supervisors showed concern for the living conditions of their workers, relations were still paternalistic. In 1819, for example, *The Times* said of Manchester workers, 'Their wretchedness seems to madden them against the rich, who they dangerously imagine engross the fruits of their labour without having any sympathy for their wants.' And in the 1840s Canon Richard Parkinson of Manchester stated, 'There is no town in the world where the distance between the rich and the poor is so great, or the barrier between them so difficult to be crossed. . . There is far less *per-*

sonal communication between the master cotton spinner and his workmen, between the calico printer and his blue-handed boys, between the master tailor and his apprentices, than there is between the Duke of Wellington and the humblest labourer on his estate.'

Helped by some of the more forward-looking businessmen, the workers of Manchester did seek to develop their integrity as a unified group. By the 1820s, for example, groups like the Manchester Mechanics' Institute (providing education and fellowship), the Footpath Preservation Society (guaranteeing access to nearby country walks important for health and recreation), and local co-operatives all offered proof of working class efforts at organisation. But simultaneously the spirit of antagonism was carried on. In 1829, for example, class alienation, low wages and unemployment led to serious local riots, and an observer noted that, as the troops advanced 'the crowds ran down the narrow lanes and passages by which the principal streets are intersected; and no sooner had the troops passed than they issued from this retreat and crowded the streets as densely as before'. Only a few years later, when Manchester's distinguished gentleman scientist, John Dalton, discoverer of the atomic theory, was presented at court to William IV, the king nervously asked him, 'How are you getting on in Manchester?' Dalton replied, 'Well, I don't know, just middlin', I think.'

If one looked at the living conditions of the least well paid cotton operatives, a description such as Dalton's was not surprising. Many workers awoke at 5 a.m., laboured in the factories from 6 a.m. to 8 a.m., took half an hour for a breakfast of tea and bread, then worked until noon. An hour was allowed for the mid-day meal, which contained little meat, and might be only boiled potatoes with lard or butter. The operatives then returned to the factory and worked until 7 p.m., perhaps later. Factory rooms were kept warm and moist (the best condition for cotton). The worker's body became covered with dust and broken pieces of cotton fibres. Many of the operations of machinery required great physical stamina, tiring the worker's body as the day proceeded. At the same time, many of the motions required were exacting and, though repeated thousands of times a day, had to be performed with almost mathematical accuracy. A break in concentration might also lead to personal injury, since few of the machines had protective guards or were designed with safety in mind. Day-to-day wear and tear on the body led, in any case, to skin problems and a wide variety of irritations of chest and throat and eyes.

Residential conditions were no better. While the middle and upperclasses might enjoy attractive houses in cleaner sections of the central city, or, increasingly, in the suburbs, workers were often segregated in low-lying areas near the Irk and Irwell where drainage was poor and smoke from factories ever present.

Until the 1840s, when local government action began to have some effects, lodgings in these districts were unhealthy. Most of the districts had no common sewers. Streets were narrow, unpaved and usually muddy because of the frequent rain as well as slops thrown from dwellings, refuse and human waste. Houses, usually of brick, built quickly by speculative builders, were mostly two-storey, laid out with no sense of 'urban planning' and no consideration of aesthetics, in long straight streets, off which ran thousands of lanes and tiny cul-de-sacs. Houses were usually back to back, leaving no room for outdoor privies. Ventilation was poor. The workers could not afford a great deal of furniture. There were also many cellar dwellings, even more damp than the first two storeys. In rooms used by recent migrants from the countryside, who retained their country ways, whole families might sleep on a single bed of straw with the pigs and dogs. In common lodging houses, which proliferated to serve migrant labourers and newcomers, bedding was sometimes changed so seldom that the filth simply accumulated until eventually a lodger protested.

Some improvement in working conditions was obtained through national action by the Factory Acts, Parliament's major device for addressing the problems of working conditions facing all British industry. The first Acts, in 1802 and 1819, applied only to cotton mills, and the Act of 1802 affected only parish apprentices. The first really significant measure came in 1833: it imposed some regulations on child labour, provided for some education, and established factory inspectors (although at first there were only four). An Act of 1844 extended protection for young people to women, regardless of age. The Act also had the effect of preventing night work by women and young people. In 1847 the so-called Ten Hours Act prohibited all young people

6   Interior of a Manchester cellar. From George R Catt, *A Pictorial History of Manchester*, 1843

and women from working more than ten hours a day and fifty-eight hours a week. In 1874 this was reduced to 56½ hours, with a further reduction in 1901 to 55½. Other Acts throughout the nineteenth century gradually improved the safety of the work environment and health conditions (e.g. the amount of steaming allowed in a room).

CHAPTER 3

The creation of public order

Orderly adjustment to expansion was not really possible until Manchester obtained efficient government. At the start of the nineteenth century no fewer than five local authorities were involved in the town's administration: a court leet, which held authority under the ancient rights of the lord of the manor; the Anglican Church Wardens and overseers who administered the poor laws, certain Church taxes, and other aspects of running the parish of Manchester; the police and the improvement commissioners, who held authority under Acts of Parliament; and the surveyors of highways and the justices of the peace who participated in the governing of the county of Lancaster (Lancashire). Competition, confusion, duplication and total failure to perform certain functions were the recurring features of this situation. Under the Police Act of 1792, for example, power to light and cleanse streets and to maintain a police force after sunset was assigned to a body of Police and Improvement Commissioners composed of a boroughreeve and constables, officials of the Collegiate Church of Manchester, and owners and occupiers of property rateable at an annual value of £30 or more. Police responsibilities for the daylight hours, however, were in the hands of the court leet, which provided two constables who served one year at a time with no pay, a deputy constable who received pay, and thirty men under the deputy. This was clearly an inadequate arrangement for keeping order in a growing industrial city.

While calls for improvement in government were voiced repeatedly, they gained momentum only gradually. In 1808, for example, a large meeting of town leaders was held at an inn in Manchester, and proposals were circulated for reform of the police force, increased parliamentary authority to repair streets, and purchase of the lord of the manor's rights and property by the township. But this movement was stymied by existing holders of local offices who did not wish to give up their power, by cautious citizens who mistrusted any kind of increase in governmental power, and many members of the rising business class who wanted to invest their money in private business rather than tax-supported improvement. Conservatives demanded more dramatic proof of the need for change in local government.

It came with a vengeance in the years after 1815. With the Napoleonic wars at an end, the problems of public order already accompanying industrial transformation were exacerbated throughout the country. Prices, which had been kept artificially high by tariffs and blockades, were not immediately lowered. Farmers and manufacturers, conditioned to the needs and opportunities of a wartime market, found difficulty in readjusting to peacetime conditions. Soldiers, thrown back into civilian life, soon increased the number of unemployed wandering through town and countryside. These developments merely added to difficulties the Manchester area was already experiencing – such as dislocation of hand-loom weavers, the shock of absorbing new migrants, extreme economic fluctuations from boom to slump, and regimentation accompanying adoption of the factory system. Thus, as early as 1812, districts in and around Manchester had been the scene of rioting, torchlight demonstrations and machine breaking by workers convinced that the new manufacturing system was turning them into an exploited class. Similar disturbances occurred in the following years. They formed the background to an event which was to make the problem of government in factory towns a national issue.

On 16th August 1819, working class unrest in Manchester reached a climax. Some 60,000 people came from all over Lancashire to meet at St Peter's Field, a partially built-up open space on the south-west edge of town. The major event of the day was to be a speech by the famous radical orator Henry Hunt (1773-1835). Expecting trouble, the local authorities had stationed special constables, under the command of magistrates, in and around the crowd. Also present were several contingents of troops, under the direction of a military commander rather than the local authorities. They included infantry detachments stationed on the outskirts of the crowd, local Yeomanry a quarter of a mile away on horseback; along with mounted Hussars and other Yeomanry half a mile away. ('Police' in the modern sense did not exist until 1829, when Sir Robert Peel established the Metropolitan force in London, with other towns and cities following thereafter). According to some interpreters, the arrangement of troops in Manchester was part of a premeditated plot to attack and disperse the assembled workers by violent means. But most surviving evidence suggests that the town authorities and the military commander intended to employ force only in stages – and only if the special constables could not handle things or the meeting seemed to pose a serious threat to public peace.

By the time Hunt was about to speak, however, several magistrates had become disturbed by the size and mood of the meeting, and they ordered the constables to arrest Hunt and others near him on the speaker's platform. Judging the crowd around Hunt to be particularly dense and unruly, the constables refused to make arrests without military assistance. To this the magistrates agreed. Hurried communication then took place between magistrates and the various contingents of troops. While it was still in progress, the mounted Yeomanry arrived at the edges of the crowd, unaccompanied by the military commander and the regular troops. There followed a hasty conference between the chief constables, the boroughreeve and the commanders of the Yeomanry – a conference which resulted in an on-the-spot decision to have the Yeomanry make the arrests immediately. The Yeomanry began to make their way into the crowd towards the speaker's platform. Evidence suggests that their progress was at first peaceful and unopposed. But by this times nerves were on edge. Suddenly a struggle began between parts of the crowd and parts of the Yeomanry. Some of the Yeomanry became isolated. Then, for reasons which have caused puzzlement to the present day, panic erupted. Men and women screamed, sabres flashed, and a full-scale riot ensued. When the dust settled and the sun began to dry the blood on the ground, some six to eleven persons had been killed and another one hundred to six hundred seriously injured. Before the day was over, news of these events was on its way to London, to England, and to the world. Parallels were immediately drawn with the recent battle of Waterloo, and the term 'Peterloo' became a part of every Englishman's vocabulary. To this day the word symbolises the most important of all the riots in nineteenth century British history, and has frequently been adopted in European history textbooks as a label for the conservative 'age of reaction' which is said to have followed the Napoleonic wars.

For an event of such note, Peterloo is still clouded in a suprising amount of ignorance. The whole question of who 'attacked' first – crowd or Yeomanry – is still the subject of intense debate. Given the present paucity of documents, it may never be fully settled. Equally perplexing are the psychological elements of the event. There was a strange mixture of holiday atmosphere, siege mentality and small-town nervousness on the day of Peterloo. The military brought not only sabres but small arms and cannon. Many citizens noted uneasily that 'strangers' from smaller textile towns in the region were joining the mob at St Peter's Field, almost as if Manchester were a medieval village gawking at visitors. Workmen carried staves and clubs for protection against possible attack, and, indeed, marched into town in almost military formation in some cases. But many brought their wives and children with them, and carried colourful, carefully embroidered banners. For example, a club of Female Reformers from Oldham carried a white silk banner decorated with shirt ruffles upon which were the phrases 'Annual Parliaments', 'Votes by Ballot' and 'Universal Suffrage'. Similarly, reformers from Rochdale marched in regular time to the sound of a bugle and carried two green banners and a cap of Liberty on a red pole, crowned with leaves of laurel and bearing the inscription 'Hunt and Liberty'. Samuel Bamford, one of the radical leaders, wrote in his memoirs, *Passages in the Life of a Radical* (1844), that he and others who marched to St Peter's Field were moved by 'a spirit of good will', and added, 'we went in the greatest hilarity and good humour, preceded by a band of music, which played national airs; and. . . our fathers, our mothers, our wives, our children, and our sweethearts were with us. . .' Such details suggest that careful analysis of surviving documents will be required, perhaps by psychologists and anthropologists, before all the factors which caused the 'massacre' can be known.

Contemporaries did agree, however, that Peterloo posed fundamental questions concerning public order. William Hulton, the conscientious Tory squire who gave the crucial order for the Yeomanry to enter the crowd, was typical in this respect. In later reflections he was to emphasise repeatedly that he never let himself forget that he was under oath to defend the laws of the realm, and at least once he asserted that the manner in which he had defended those laws made 16th August 1819 'the proudest day in his life'. Other observers maintained that Peterloo had been a violation not only of legal but of divine order. Contemporary comment included numerous references to the 'crucifixion' which had taken place at 'the Field of St Peter' – what was crucified, and by whom, depending on one's political sentiments. Percy Bysse Shelley, for example, rapidly revised his poem *The Mask of Anarchy,* when the news reached him on his travels in Greece, and argued in the new draft that the blood spilt on 16th August had been a redemptive sacrifice for the liberal cause. Similarly, in 1832, the *Manchester Guardian* quoted the following parody on the Litany which had been circulating for some time:

> From all those damnable bishops, lords and peers, –
> from all those bloody murdering Peterloo butchers –
> from all those idle drones that live out of the earning
> of the people – Good Lord deliver us.

It was likewise possible in the years after 1819 to find people owning scarves, lockets, or tobacco boxes decorated with commemorative scenes of Peterloo, much in the manner of religious trinkets. And radicals, particularly, marked the anniversary of the event. In a newspaper account of the eleventh anniversary meeting in 1830, at which Henry Hunt was present, it was reported: 'When the procession arrived in Peter Street, and near to the field of blood, the whole multitude halted. Mr. Hunt requested the men to take off their hats – the band commenced playing the 'Dead March in Saul', and the carriages were slowly drawn, as close as possible to the place where the hustings stood on that never-to-be-forgotten day. . .'

Reminders of Peterloo were also provided by journalists, who continued to refer to the event in articles about local government throughout the 1820s. Perhaps the most far-reaching efforts of this kind were made by John Edward Taylor (1791-1844), a

7 'A representation of the Manchester Reform Meeting dispersed by
the Civil and Military Power, Aug. 16th 1819'

young Manchester cotton merchant. His concern led him first
to a careful investigation of the causes of Peterloo and eventually, in 1821 to the founding of his own paper, the *Manchester
Guardian* (see *below,* pp. 187-192) out of conviction that a
paucity of information about questions of local government had
been the major reason for the tragedy.

The subject of Peterloo was also debated in Parliament, and
for many years after the event there was demand for an official
inquiry. In fact, no such inquiry was ever held. The government
argued that none was needed and saw the legal prosecutions
which had followed the event as sufficient opportunity for
inquiry.

But the efforts of concerned local people such as John Edward
Taylor did gradually increase understanding of the problems
which Peterloo had dramatised, so that by the end of the 1820s
the foundations were finally laid for change in Manchester's old

ways of local government. In the early 1830s Parliament's introduction of the First Reform Bill provided the opportunity which
Manchester reformers had been seeking. The Reform Bill proposed to extend the franchise to £10 householders and to reap-
portion the membership of the House of Commons, with slightly
increased representation for growing cities. In Manchester, as
elsewhere, the measure prompted excited debate. Despite opposition from Manchester Tories, a meeting expressing support,
involving some 100,000 citizens, was organised by Thomas
Potter and Abel Heywood, and a petition advocating passage of
the Reform Bill, with 24,000 signatures, was taken by coach to
London, covering the distance in a record-breaking seventeen
hours. This excitement, and the subsequent election, in 1833,
of the town's first two Members of Parliament, Mark Philips
and Charles Poulett Thomson, greatly increased Manchester's
concern for the quality of its local government. The same was
true of Salford, which also received one parliamentary seat by
the Reform Act of 1832, won by Joseph Brotherton.

Another major change in local government came in 1835 when
Parliament passed the Municipal Corporations Act. Thomas
Potter, William Neild, John Edward Taylor and Richard Cobden
led a campaign for a charter of incorporation for the parliamentary borough of Manchester. In spite of vigorous opposition this
resulted, in late 1838, in official acceptance of a charter incor-
porating the townships of Manchester, Cheetham, Hulme,
Ardwick, Chorlton on Medlock and Beswick – which, together
had a population of some 242,000. In the same year, Manchester
elected its first mayor, Thomas Potter. Over the next four years
the charter continued to be opposed by Tories, who claimed that
it was based on a technically incorrect interpretation of Parliament's intent and did not represent the sentiment of a majority
of ratepayers. But this problem was removed in 1842 by the
Borough Charters Incorporation Act (which performed the same
function for Birmingham and Bolton, where similar controver-
sies had arisen). Then in 1846 a major step was taken when the
Corporation of Manchester bought out the manorial rights of
the Mosley family for £200,000. This cleared the way for efficient
local government by the borough council (composed of sixteen
aldermen and forty-eight councillors) and Manchester's brilliant young town clerk, Joseph Heron.

CHAPTER 4

Social Reform

Government gave Victorian Manchester the rudiments of public order. But the city also needed social services – to use a modern term – if problems of industrial growth were to be addressed adequately.

The Nonconformist conscience. To understand how these services delevoped, one must look first at the religious life of Manchester, because that was the source of the energies which prompted social reform and defined its character.

Almost every writer on the industrial revolution has noticed that the scientists, inventors, manufacturers, merchants, and bankers who played leading roles in the industrial revolution included a large percentage of Baptists, Congregationalists, Presbyterians, Quakers, Unitarians and members of other dissenting sects outside the Anglican Church. This was true of Manchester as well. Here, as in other cities, Nonconformity carried a number of advantages. Foremost was the incentive to *work,* proceeding from the 'Protestant ethic'. Dissenters were also united by networks of social reliability. As in the case of Jews and Huguenots on the Continent, religion was an incentive to trust among those of similar faith. It provided a means of passing on vital information about business conditions – whether at meeting houses and chapels or through family contacts resulting from intermarriage. Dissent could also foster originality, since it attracted those who would challenge accepted ways, and it could intensify the will to succeed as a means of dealing with forces of oppression. Finally, there were educational advantages. From the late seventeenth century onwards, dissenters had been forced to set up their own schools, since adherence to official Church doctrine was required for attendance at Anglican institutions (which even included Oxford and Cambridge until the 1850s).

These schools were particularly distinguished for training in science and the more practical disciplines, partly because of conscious desire to offer an alternative to the literary education emphasised at Church schools and at Oxford and Cambridge, and partly because the Nonconformist view of the world was more comfortable with an empirical approach to knowledge which emphasised each person's reliance upon reason and the five senses instead of automatic adherence to abstract doctrines of faith.

While Nonconformity gave advantages to those who competed in the industrial revolution, it also produced extremes of con science in those who succeeded. Many dissenters, once they had won the battle for wordly success, judged those who had fallen behind in the race harshly. Lack of success was presumed to result from sinful lack of self-discipline and was often taken as proof of Calvin's doctrine that many born into life were predestined to suffering in this world and to damnation in the afterlife. In contrast to Anglicans, Nonconformists of this persuasion were notable for a lack of sympathy and a reluctance to support charities which did not place strict demands upon the receiver of aid. Other Nonconformists were less fatalistic, however. They emphasised the Protestant insistence upon individual initiative and ability to think for oneself. To dissenters of this persuasion it seemed logical that intelligent appeals to the reason and common sense of the unfortunate would lead to the redemption of many. Unlike Anglicans and Catholics, who tended to see misery as inevitable and who viewed the poor as almost saintly sufferers likely to be rewarded in the next life, Nonconformists of an activist persuasion searched for new methods of social engineering which would eradicate problems traceable to human lack of will and failure to use God-given intelligence.

Manchester possessed influential citizens who were guided by both extremes of the Nonconformist conscience. Those of stern outlook were the ones who insisted that workers' wages be kept low; that hours should not be reduced; that workers should help themselves rather than seek aid from others. Of the many examples of the harshness which such merchants and factory owners imposed upon Manchester, perhaps the most visible was the neglect of provision for attractive green spaces in which masters and men could share moments away from the factories. Almost no merchant or manufacturer had the generosity to donate valuable land in the centre of the city for this purpose, even though Liverpool, for example, showed more enlightened town planning. In 1833 a visiting factory inspector reported, 'It is impossible not to notice the total absence of public gardens, parks, and walks at Manchester: it is scarcely in the power of the factory workman to taste the breath of nature or to look upon its verdure, and this defect is a strong impediment to convalescence from disease, which is usually tedious and difficult at Manchester.'

On the other hand, Manchester also possessed a significant number of Nonconformists who worked to improve social conditions. To understand the city, it is important to look at their efforts. Modern commentators sometimes convey the impression that nineteenth century industrialists and merchants showed sensitivity to their workers only when pushed by measures such as the Factory Acts. While there is a great deal of truth in this view, one should also acknowledge that local residents often took the lead in attacking problems long before Parliament acted.

In the case of Manchester, the headquarters of such activity was the Cross Street Chapel, the major gathering place of Unitarians in the city. The chapel's influence was due to a number of factors: a succession of dynamic ministers going back to the eighteenth century; stability in chapel governance; strategic location near the very centre of the city; and the notably high educational level of members, many of whom were graduates of Warrington Academy – half-way between Liverpool and Manchester along the River Mersey – which was particularly distinguished for training in science.

Teachers from Warrington established Manchester New College, which held its first classes at Cross Street Chapel, while many members of the Manchester Literary and Philosophical Society received their training at Warrington as well. Before 1830 Unitarians had founded at least three elementary schools in Manchester, a Natural History Society, one of the town's Mechanics' Institutes, and the first art gallery. Many Manchester citizens also obtained their first training in public speaking at Cross Street Chapel, including Richard Cobden and eight other men who were later to become MPs.

Medical Reform. Social reforms traceable to Cross Street Chapel were an important part of Manchester's development from the 1830s onward. For example, the public health movement took a giant step forward nationally in that decade owing to the efforts of a young member of the congregation. The stimulus for this reform came in spring 1832, when cholera struck Liverpool, Leeds, Sheffield, Glasgow, London and a number of other towns, including Manchester. A terse report of 29th May 1832, from the case files of one Manchester doctor, showed how devastating such an epidemic could be.

'No. 4, *Elizabeth Cavanagh,* aged 36, – Residence, 5, Wakefield-street, Little Ireland, ground floor. Employment, mother of preceding. Constitution, healthy looking hearty woman. Natural susceptibility, had often had severe diarrhoea especially when suckling her children. Predisposing cause, half starved; got nothing but potatoes and tea when she had her meals at home, was brutally treated by the man with whom she cohabited. Exciting cause, fatigue from attending and grief for the loss of her child No. 3. Locality, crowding, filth, etc. . . Cavanagh's house. . . fronted an open area but an impure stream whose channel does the function of a sewer, passes by the door to an adjoining field where it collects and stagnates: house and inhabitants very filthy: three children and two adults sleeping on a straw bed. . . Communication or non-communication, as she was getting out of bed on Monday night to reach the basin for her child No. 3, he vomited upon her and part of the vomit entered her mouth. Soon after her seizure she mentioned the circumstance to her neighbour Mrs. Featherstone, adding she was taken exactly as her child had been.'

Since the Middle Ages England had suffered almost annually from epidemics which led to ravages of this kind. Many were probably outbreaks of dysentery and flu. By the late eighteenth century medical literature had begun to mention 'Asiatic cholera' as well, a particularly virulent sickness which frequently devastated the Army in India and led to riots and panic. Medical understanding of the disease was limited, and only in the mid nineteenth century were scientists able to learn that cholera is almost always transmitted by connecting links between infected human excrement and the mouths of susceptible persons, and that, given a common water supply, it can infect and kill thousands of people with terrifying suddenness and then, in non-endemic areas, die out just as suddenly because of the fragility of the bacteria. Efficient sewers, purified drinking water and minimal standards of cleanliness are usually enough to eradicate it from any community. In 1832, however, these facts were only vaguely understood and there were good grounds for predicting that doctors would see themselves as helpless.

But in a few of the larger industrial cities, including Manchester, local governmental authorities fought back by setting up Special Boards of Health, mobilising the talents of individual doctors and drawing upon the knowledge of amateur scientific societies. Manchester's first board of health, in existence since the 1790s, had been set up to deal with a typhus epidemic. The new special board, established in anticipation of an epidemic in November 1831, when cholera reached central Europe from Asia, was an adjunct to this body.

Its greatest asset was its secretary, Dr James P. Kay, an earnest, hardworking young physician and regular worshipper at Cross Street Chapel, whose performance during subsequent months was to bring him national fame. Like so many of the most influential medical men in Scotland and the north of England, Kay had studied at the University of Edinburgh Medical School under Professor William P. Alison, the man who almost singlehandedly alerted an entire generation of doctors to the connections between urban life and disease. Kay had worked for several years in what he called the 'wynds, closes, and barrack-houses' of Edinburgh Old Town, and had spent an autumn among the poor in Dublin – both experiences increasing his sympathy for downtrodden Celtic populations. He had also visited the major cities of Europe. Gradually he became convinced that the condition of most of the urban poor was more often rectifiable than it was inevitable. In 1827 he applied for a position as surgeon at the Royal Infirmary in Manchester. Failing in that application, he obtained the position of medical officer at the recently opened Ardwick and Ancoats Dispensary, an understaffed facility housed in a shoddy brick building in the factory and tenement districts on the eastern side of the city. Daily contact with the workers he treated there strengthened Kay's belief in the connections between ill health and poor environment – a belief which he had been stating to friends for some years before 1831, and which he had recently begun to propagate in medical journals, at least one of which he helped to found.

Kay and other backers of the special board had originally hoped for broad powers and extensive financial support, but Manchester's town authorities gave them far less of each than they needed. This was perhaps understandable, given the distrust in that era of anything which could be construed as governmental encroachment into the private sphere. For this reason the achievements of the Manchester special board were always inadequate, but the key point is that they were less inadequate than the efforts of other towns. G. M. Young, writing in 1936, after close investigation of surviving documents, said that Manchester's special board proved more efficient in meeting the challenge of cholera than any other local agency in Britain.

The first step in counter-attack was systematic gathering of information. Older facilities in the town, such as the Royal Infirmary and the Ancoats Dispensary, were told to keep their eyes open for any cases which might be cholera. Doctors, charity workers, priests, ministers and others who worked regularly with the poor were asked to report strange cases of sickness. Each day the special board received news of the epidemic's progress: from Sunderland to Edinburgh, to Glasgow and to London, to Liverpool, and then up the string of small towns along the Mersey and Irwell. Some hope was placed on the device of cholera watches, though these were usually very feeble. No one at all was sent to check all the train passengers who arrived daily in Manchester, and only two regular officers were appointed to observe the canals and river ports of the area, even though doctors at that time knew in a general way that cholera was often transmitted by water. In other respects, however, the special board was more efficient. It kept in close touch with the public health authorities of Liverpool, and tried to learn from that town's harbour personnel about the means by which epidemics tended to spread. In March 1832 the special board began regular sittings. One result of these meetings was the commencement of a few surveys of the worst parts of town, where even the vaguest understanding of the connections between disease and filth was enough to make the potential for epidemic obvious. On the basis of these surveys the special board issued warnings to landlords and to local government officials that certain areas of Manchester needed to be cleaned, paved and sewered, or else evacuated immediately. Only a very few of those contacted ever followed these warnings – grim proof that the backers of the special board, for all their vigour, were always an enlightened minority.

When the cholera finally struck, in May 1832, the board set up three special cholera hospitals in Manchester in abandoned factories and warehouses, at which roughly half of all cases were eventually received; the rest were treated at home, as was the procedure with all cases in Salford. Pressure of finances was always extreme, and the facilities for treatment were never adequate. Again, however, it must be remembered that Manchester was far ahead of most other towns – even Liverpool, where the epidemic took a greater toll and where more extensive experience in treating the epidemics of a harbour city might have prompted a more vigorous response.

Careful reports were made on virtually every appearance of the disease. Dr Kay himself visited at least the first two hundred cases and kept precise notes on most of them. Manchester newspapers helped by publishing accounts of emergency meetings; they also printed weekly lists of the toll of the epidemic, usually with assurances that all would soon be well if people simply kept their heads.

As the cholera continued to spread, medical men gradually developed a routine for treatment. Something like a 'grape vine' was established, so that doctors could get word of a case immediately. Their first step was to decide whether a new victim of the disease could be left at home. If this was inadvisable, he or she was immediately taken to one of the special hospitals, where attendants tried with varying degrees of skill to lessen pain by whatever methods seemed appropriate. In all instances the special board saw to it that the victim's home was fumigated and whitewashed. Above all, the need was stressed to clean away filth and not to panic.

None of these measures, of course, was adequate, and throughout the summer the number of cases continued to increase. On
2nd September 1832 widespread fear finally broke loose when
the temporary cholera hospital in Swan Street became the scene
of a riot. Joined by a crowd which had gathered in response to
wild rumours that patients were being killed by doctors, the
inmates broke down the doors of the hospital, wrecked the beds
and other facilities in the wards, carried fellow patients away
to their homes, and narrowly avoided killing several medical
personnel. Only when the military arrived did the mob disperse.

The city was finally freed of its epidemic when cold weather
arrived in mid-October. Most townsmen would have preferred
to forget the entire summer's experience. But the medical reformers had other ideas. Although the special board was soon dis-
banded, it did issue a small pamphlet, entitled *The Moral and
Physical Condition of the Working Classes of Manchester in
1832,* published in London in that year. Other works had dis
cussed the strictly medical features of the cholera. This pamphlet was intended to be the special board's chief means for
dealing with the social questions the epidemic had raised. Based
upon numerous sources, the pamphlet was in one sense the work
of many hands. But the major author was J. P. Kay. He fused
disparate facts into a work of sociological genius that was soon
to influence the thinking of an entire nation.

To understand the power which Kay's pamphlet exerted upon
readers of his day, one must abstract the vision which it
imparted. Kay asked readers to note the similarities between
a great city and the human body. Both were wondrously complete creations; both divided their general activities into more
particular functions; both carried out these functions by means
of sectors marvellously adapted to their special purposes; both
required that the needs of various sectors be communicated to
co-ordinating agencies which could determine how to meet such
needs; and both would die if the diseases accumulating in one
sector were allowed to endure and to spread without detection
to others. Modern urban sociologists might depreciate the value
of this organic analogy; there are dangers in trying to base public policy on the assumption that a city is a living being. At the
dawn of the Victorian age, however, such a comparison was
highly effective. Kay's parallel made readers' fears for the wel-

8   *The Moral and Physical Condition of the Working Classes of
Manchester in 1832* by Dr James P Kay

only, we discover in those districts which contain a large portion of poor, namely, in Nos. 1, 2, 3, 4, 7, 10, 13, and 14, that among 579 streets inspected, 243 were altogether unpaved—46 partially paved—93 ill ventilated—and 307 contained heaps of refuse, deep ruts, stagnant pools, ordure, &c.; and in the districts which are almost exclusively inhabited by the poor, namely, Nos. 1, 2, 3, 4, and 10, among 438 streets inspected, 214 were altogether unpaved—32 partially paved—63 ill ventilated—and 259 contained heaps of refuse, deep ruts, stagnant pools, ordure, &c.

The replies to the questions proposed in the second table relating to houses, contain equally remarkable results, which have been carefully arranged by the Classification Committee of the Special Board of Health, as follows.

District	No. of houses inspected.	No. of houses reported as requiring whitewashing	No. of houses reported as requiring repair.	No. of houses in which the soughs wanted repair.	No. of houses damp.	No. of houses reported as ill ventilated.	No. of houses wanting privies.
1	850	399	128	112	177	70	326
2	2489	898	282	145	497	109	755
3	213	145	104	41	61	52	96
4	650	279	106	105	134	69	250
5	413	176	82	70	101	11	66
6	12	3	5	5			5
7	343	76	59	57	86	21	79
8	132	35	30	39	48	22	20
9	128	34	32	24	39	19	25
10	370	195	53	123	54	2	232
11							
12	113	33	23	27	24	16	52
13	757	218	44	108	146	54	177
14	481	74	13	83	68	7	138
Total ..	6951	2565	960	939	1435	452	2221

It is however to be lamented, that even these numerical results fail to exhibit a perfect picture of the ills which are suffered by the poor. The replies fare of society synonymous with their fears about preservation of their own bodies.

The next step in his argument was dissection. In the case of Manchester and other cities, he told his readers, few men yet understood the underlying social causes of the patient's symptoms. The first need was to look below the surface. But to an author and an audience raised in the puritan tradition this prospect was upsetting. No more than they wished to expose their own bodily parts did they wish to discuss the underside of city life, even though some might know its workings in detail. Kay himself was subject to such upset, as when his report referred to 'excrementitious matter'. In the main, however, he must have known that he would gain by his honesty in face of offensive details. Though the terms were not his, one may say that he sensed he was speaking to long repressed fears about city life – fears whose powers could be judged by the mere fact that they had been so repressed. Two passages from the report illustrate how Kay played upon such sensibilities:

'In some districts of the town exist evils so remarkable as to require more minute description. A portion of low, swampy ground, liable to be frequently inundated, and to constant exhalation, is included between a high bank over which the Oxford Road passes, and a bend of the river Medlock, where its course is impeded by a weir. . . This district has sometimes been the haunt of hordes of thieves and desperadoes who defied the law, and is always inhabited by a class resembling savages in their appetites and habits. It is surrounded on every side by some of the largest factories of the town, whose chimneys vomit forth dense clouds of smoke, which hang heavily over this insalubrious region.'

'Near the centre of town, a mass of buildings, inhabited by prostitutes and thieves, is intersected by narrow and loathsome streets, and close courts defiled with refuse. . . In Parliament-street there is only one privy for three hundred and eighty inhabitants, which is placed in a narrow passage, whence its effluvia infest the adjacent houses, and must prove a fertile source of disease.'

Another writer might have been more clinical in his descriptions and could have said that the way to treat problems of the type discussed was simply to find the cause and then remove it.

That has often been the approach to urban difficulties in more recent times. But, living in a religiously oriented age, Kay wanted to convince his readers that the scientific category of 'disease' and the theological category of 'evil' were the same. Thus, like the above-quoted passages, his entire report evoked a subconscious sense of Manichean struggle between the forces of light and the forces of darkness. For Kay and his readers, doctors and those who sided with them became the heroes in this struggle, and general ignorance and improvidence the enemies.

To the extent that Kay's report led people to regard riot, crime, sickness, prostitution and horrible living conditions as resulting from lack of knowledge, publicly supported popular education was seen as the cure – and from the late 1830s on Kay was to devote the major portion of his life to this cause.

But the major effects of his report were upon the national movement for public health measures. Public response was not like the huge sensation which would come several years later when Sir John Simon's reports as chief medical officer in London, just after the cholera epidemic of 1849, were discussed and reprinted throughout the realm. Nearly two decades of intense political activity had to intervene before the subject of public health could arouse such interest. Kay's report marked the beginning rather than the culmination of this movement. But it filled an important gap.

Although a national Board of Health had been formed to deal with the cholera epidemic, it had left no official report, unless one would include in that category a few pieces of paper upon which one of the central board's officers had scrawled a few relevant figures, and which were later found shut away with the personal belongings of King William IV. Clearly the nation as a whole lacked Manchester's sense of the value of systematic investigation. Thus the information made public by Kay's pamphlet was, as G. M. Young said, 'one of the cardinal documents of Victorian history. For the first time the condition of a great urban population was exposed to view.'

Correctly or incorrectly, people saw 'no reason to suppose that Manchester was any worse than other towns, and the inevitable conclusion was that an increasing portion of the population of England was living under conditions which were not only a

negation of civilized existence, but a menace to civilized society'
(Young). Kay's report became a classic overnight; the information it imparted has been called 'perhaps the most fruitful
quarry for social reforms in the 1830s and 1840s. . .' (M. W.
Flinn). Kay's report also inspired another Manchester resident,
Edwin Chadwick, who became active in public health work in
London and throughout Britain, and who, more than any other
single figure, was to be responsible for publicising 'the sanitary
idea' throughout Britain. Writing in the early 1840s, at about
the time when he published his famous *Report on the Sanitary
Condition of the Labouring Population of Great Britain* (1842),
Chadwick reflected on his colleague's crucial role in earlier days:

'One of his [Kay's] first conspicuous acts of practical Christ-
ianity as a young man was to examine the state of the residences
of the poor and helpless of the labouring classes in Manchester:
to call attention to the sources of the pestilence and of the evils
which had hitherto fallen upon the poor but industrious artisan
like the arrow that flieth in the dark. The pamphlet of Dr Kay
on the condition of the labouring classes in Manchester was the
precursor of the most beneficial course of enquiry in modern
times as to the sanitary condition of the labouring classes in
respect to the surrounding physical circumstances of defective
drainage and the condition of their residences now in progress
throughout the country.'

But the most important consequence of Kay's report was that
it helped to hasten a major shift in national attitude. As G. M.
Young has written, 'perhaps the first step towards dealing effec-
tively with slums was to recognise them as slums and not as
normal phenomena of urban existence'. The medical reformers
of Manchester were one of the first groups in the world to make
this shift in outlook and to persuade others of its value.

The industrial city quantified. Another nationally important response to urban problems of the early Victorian era was
Manchester's great interest in 'statistics', recently grown from
what had been called political or social arithmetic into one of
the most popular studies of the day. 'It is indeed truly said,' the
council of the Statistical Society of London declared in 1838,
'that the spirit of the present age has an evident tendency to
confront the figures of speech with the figures of arithmetic; it

being impossible not to observe a growing distrust of mere hypothetical theory and *a priori* assumption, and the appearance of a general conviction that, in the business of social science, principles are valid for application only inasmuch as they are legitimate deductions from facts, accurately observed and methodically classified. . .' The sources of this spirit could be found well before the 1830s. Reynolds, Child, Petty, Price, Arthur Young, Chalmers, Playfair, Adam Smith and Bentham had all helped to develop it. More recently it had been evident in McCulloch's *Dictionary of Commerce* (1832) and Marshall's *Digest* (1833), while it was soon to be embodied in Porter's famous *Progress of the Nation* (1836-43). Manchester played an important part in this nationwide movement. In 1832 a Statistical Office was set up at the Board of Trade in London, chiefly due to the efforts of Lord Auckland and of C. E. Poulett Thomson, MP for Manchester. In 1833 the British Association, meeting in Cambridge, established a statistical section; then, in the autumn of 1833, only a short time after, Manchester founded its own Statistical Society. Because the event preceded by some months the founding of a Statistical Society in London (later known as the Royal Statistical Society), Manchester has possessed ever since the oldest continuously existing statistical society in Britain.

The idea of founding a Manchester Statistical Society was chiefly the inspiration of William Langton (b. 1803), a cashier at Heywood's Bank. The son of a Preston merchant, Langton had studied and travelled in Europe while still a young man, and then, at the age of eighteen, had gone into business as a commercial agent for English firms in Russia. In Liverpool he became involved with the Provident Society organised by Elizabeth Fry, which taught workers practical ethics through discussion of the Bible and helped them to place part of their wages in savings accounts. In 1829 he moved to Manchester, where he helped to found the District Provident Society. His work as the society's secretary soon made him feel the need for some systematic means of collecting information about social conditions. He broached his ideas to his friend and fellow secretary, Dr J. P. Kay. A short while later Kay was on tour in Derbyshire with two friends, the factory owners Samuel and William Rathbone Greg, when he presented Langton's ideas for their criticisms.

The reaction of the two brothers was quite in line with their background. Both had inherited deep social concern from their father, Samuel Greg, a leading cotton manufacturer who had migrated from Belfast to set up the Quarry Bank mill and a model workers' village at Styal, south-west of Manchester in 1784. His first son, Samuel, born in 1804, was educated at Unitarian schools and spent a session at the University of Edinburgh. The younger Samuel developed and amplified the family interest in the improving features of industry, and in 1832 he was given the opportunity to apply his convictions when he assumed supervision of Lower House Mill in Bollington. Here he built a model village which included playing fields, a Sunday school, a library and evening classes for 300 workers and their dependants. The village ran smoothly until 1846, when a dispute with the workers forced him to retire until his death in 1876.

Samuel's younger brother, William, born in Manchester in 1809, was even more interested in social questions. In 1828, after education on a pattern similar to Samuel's, he became manager of a mill his father owned in Bury, and in 1832 he set up his own cotton business in Manchester.

The tour through Derbyshire with J. P. Kay was followed some days later by a meeting at the home of Benjamin Heywood, where plans for the District Provident Society had previously taken shape. Heywood agreed to provide financial backing for the statistical society and soon began to recruit additional support from influential friends. Funds thus became available for provisional operations, and the Manchester Statistical Society held its first meeting, at Heywood's house, on 2nd September, 1833. Thirteen persons were in attendance. They described themselves as a group of 'gentlemen accustomed for the most part to meet in private society, and whose habits and opinions are not uncongenial'. Cotton manufacturers, clergymen, Nonconformist ministers, medical men and bankers were represented. All were under forty, all were interested in philanthropy, all had a strong literary bent; all were closely connected with local business life; all, even when they were not actually Unitarians, were closely connected with Cross Street Chapel; and all would be described today, relative to other Manchester

9   Quarry Bank Mill, Styal

groups, as moderately liberal in politics, religion and temperament. None of the town's 'Tories' was represented, and none of
the 'radicals'.

The founders had several reasons for organising the society.
Statistics could disclose previously unseen or little emphasised
relationships, lighting up the social problems that had been
discovered and perhaps giving a sense of mastery of the situation. Secondly, statistics could be used to further the cause of
social reform. It provided 'evidence' upon which the legal case
for change could be argued. Finally, it seems likely that statistics held a 'magical' fascination. Interest in the religious and
mystical importance of numbers had waned and intensified in
Western civilisation ever since ancient times, and the Victorian
era, as many writers have shown, was a time when such interest
was very strong.

In the case of the founders of the Manchester Statistical
Society this general spirit took an unmistakably religious form.
The society's chief goal, in effect, was a census of lost souls. This
much could be seen clearly in its choice of topics for investigation. Unlike some statistical groups elsewhere in Britain, the
Manchester society determined never to discuss purely abstract
matters relating to mathematics or science. Questions of industrial relations in the purely business sense were also excluded,
and it is notable that the society never yielded to the temptation
to study only the textile industry. Even issues of party politics
were officially omitted, though the convictions of individual
members did of course shine through from time to time. The
living conditions among the lower classes of Manchester was
repeatedly stated, from the very day of founding, as the society's
prime concern. Even the middle and upper classes were dealt
with only for comparative purposes.

So clear in their purposes were the founders, indeed, that it
took them only until their fourth meeting, on 15th January
1834, to define the scope of their inquiries for the next seven
years. It was agreed that there was little chance of the government adopting any nationwide system of statistical inquiry, so
that the Manchester society might well fill some important gaps.
Thus particular attention should be paid to 'the command which
in a right state of moral feeling the working classes have over
the necessaries of life', and to this end a statistical classification

of the city's inhabitants would be immensely helpful. Data on
the costs of food and clothing would be important; and 'the com-
sumption of butchers' meat in Manchester would, in connection
with that of ardent spirits, form an excellent test of the manner
in which the earnings of the poor are expended, and of the degree
in which frugality and forethought prevails'. An analysis of the
distribution and appeal of cheap books and pamphlets would be
a good way to learn more about 'the opinion and the state of
feelings in the lower orders'; commercial expansion in the Manchester area might be discovered by compiling lists of the horse-
power used in local mills and by finding the tonnage of products
carried by canal craft and railway waggons during given years.
To this report of the conversation Dr Kay himself added that
the society should appoint a sub-committee to analyse the recent
report of the Factory Commissioners who had worked with
Michael Sadler's parliamentary committee of inquiry; the
statistics in that volume might well provide valuable information about wages and profits in the Manchester area. Dr Kay
also noted that Poulett Thomson had promised to provide the
society with information secured by parliamentary commissions
on the subject of popular education.

    To carry out this programme the Manchester Statistical
Society set up one of the best systems of inquiry in existence.
The nucleus was the society's small, and always rather clubby
circle of personally acquainted members. Meetings were almost
always in private homes. The original membership of thirteen
was never allowed to expand beyond fifty until after 1837, in
spite of great demand from without. Within a few months after
the founding of the society the annual membership fee was fixed
at the relatively high rate of two guineas. Proposed members
were elected by ballot and could be excluded by two black balls.
They also normally had to pass the scrutiny of Benjamin
Heywood; because he personally financed so much of the
society's work, he was allowed to assert his personal preferences
as regards membership.

    In a group (though usually not at their formal meetings) the
members of the society first mapped out a general area of study
relating to one of the aspects of working class life touched upon
at the fourth meeting. Then, in a kind of seller-buyer pattern,
the group offered the question to be taken up by some member

from its ranks, who then usually took the lead in forming a committee to study it. Subordinate problems were then formulated and investigative tasks parcelled out to the committee's members. Finally the actual 'leg work' began.

The society always preferred its survey to be based on personally conducted house-to-house inquiries. 'Go and *ask* people' is a good summary of its attitude. And to this end individual members did indeed do a certain amount of canvassing. But they were busy men, and a few were undoubtably rather too chary of entering certain parts of town, so they usually procured agents with close contacts in the working class districts. Though a few of these agents were volunteers, most were paid, and a survey conducted by a single committee of the society could be expensive, costs in 1835, for example, ranging between £42 and £175 for one survey. Benjamin Heywood was the main source of such funds, though the proprietors of the cotton firm McConnell & Kennedy, both members of the society, also contributed a major share. To build respect for its agents, the society often prepared the way by distributing printed circulars announcing that they were coming. Investigators were then given whatever forms the committee had developed and went forth to fill in the blanks.

Although most of the required statistics could be collected in a routine manner, obstacles soon appeared. The Society once provoked the wrath of local Anglicans, for example, when it began to ask questions about matters of education and charity work which Church officials were themselves exploring. Class mistrust, similarly, was a major difficulty; on one occasion workers threatened and refused to aid an Irish weaver from their own part of town who had been hired because of his reliability and intelligence. There were other motives besides class, of course, which led to a desire to cover up facts. On one occasion an agent of the society was asking a local schoolmaster about the quality of his establishment. The schoolmaster immediately began to enumerate the various subjects with which he was familiar: hydraulics, hydrostatics, geography, geology, entomology and etymology. The agent referred back to his questionnaire, and asked, 'Do you teach Reading and Writing? – Yes! Arithmetic? – Yes! Grammar and Composition? – Certainly! French? – Yes! Latin? – Yes! Greek? – Yes, yes!

Geography? – Yes!' After exhausting all the inquiries on his
form the agent remarked, 'This is *multum in parvo* indeed,' to
which the schoolmaster quickly replied, 'Yes, I teach that: you
may put that down too.'

Investigators knew quite well that many of the 'facts' they
collected – such as the 'condition' of a dwelling – were quite
subjective. They were also quite aware that their technique of
statistical sampling might lead to distortions. To guard against
these difficulties, reliance was placed not upon the mathematical safeguards used by modern research groups, but upon
the 'feel' for Manchester and the surrounding area which all
the society's members possessed in abundance. Each committee
would circulate a preliminary, informal report to all the society's
members, taking note of anyone's suspicions that the conclusions went against the grain. Usually the document would then
be supplemented from this large fund of random knowledge. If
the report was well done, the society had it published, first in
its *Transactions* and then usually in reprints.

Admittedly this method had limits. The society as a whole
reflected the bias of Manchester's upper middle class. Radicals
could fault the group for failing to see that some aspects of
working class life could not change unless more basic, structural
aspects of Manchester itself were changed. The society's
writings also reflect a condescending attitude towards those it
interviewed, and no one considered inviting working class
people to meetings. The group reposed too much faith in
statistics as a panacea. Although members were well informed
about their city, they had by the late 1830s become impressed
with the depth of the problems under investigation and resigned
themselves to the need for a great deal more specialised inquiry.
Soon statistics became a hobby, and members pursued inquiries
in fields well outside the original topic of working class
conditions. At the sessions of 1837-38, for example, one delivered
a paper on 'The Past and Present Numbers of Aborigines in the
British Colonies', while the range of topics had become so wide
by 1842 that papers could be delivered on the medical statistics
of the negro race, the geology of Manchester and 'Early
Marriages in Oriental Countries as evidence of Early Puberty'.

The society nevertheless exerted great influence upon local
and national life throughout the mid-Victorian era. Because it

was a private group, not given to the parliamentary method of public inquiry before an imposing committee, it could choose topics which the government could explore only in limited ways. People would tell private investigators things they would not tell anyone armed with the power of the law. Locally, there were several results. One was an advance of interest in public education. Three members of the society played a crucial part in the founding, in 1835, of an important forum for public discussion known as the Manchester Athenaeum. A paper read at a meeting of the society in 1836 was one of the earliest proposals for a university in Manchester. And the sheer fund of data which the society collected on the topic of education made the issue a matter of greatly increased concern.

The society also exerted national influence because of the assumption, mentioned already, that conditions in Manchester were an index of conditions in the rest of the country. For this reason, reports of the society were often read before national meetings of the British Association for the Advancement of Science; many were also printed in that group's nationally circulated periodical, *The Athenaeum*. First-hand dissemination of the society's findings took place by means of the many 'corresponding members' recruited over the years. Such contacts led to the founding of new groups on the Manchester model. Evidence suggests that such was the case with the statistical societies founded in Ulster and Birmingham; it was definitely the case with the London society, founded in 1834. To these could be added the many local governmental bodies in other towns which either imitated or used the resources of the Manchester society. Edinburgh did the most extensive borrowing on both counts. Bury, Bolton, Liverpool and York all went so far as to invite members of the Manchester society to study their towns.

The society's greatest influence was upon Parliament. Its reports were quoted on the floor of the House and also greatly influenced parliamentary investigative committees. As early as 1834 they forced Michael Sadler and the Factory Act investigators to modify their perspective. From 1837 on, their data greatly influenced educational reform. And it is the opinion of some scholars that national reform in public health was largely based on data supplied by the Statistical Society until the early 1840s, when the work of J. P. Kay, Edwin Chadwick and other Manchester figures had been synthesised into the national debate.

By that time many social and economic investigators had undertaken studies throughout Britain, focusing not only on the cotton industry but upon conditions involved in the manufacture of wool, steel, iron and other products. Examples included J. C. Symons, *Arts and Artisans at Home and Abroad* (1839); W. P. Alison, *Observations on the Management of the Poor in Scotland and its Effects on the Health of Great Towns* (1840); Thomas Carlyle, *Past and Present* (1843); James Leach, *Stubborn Facts from the Factories* (1844); and numerous parliamentary reports.

Manchester and 'the social question' abroad. By the 1830s the immense productive force of Manchester had made it a required stop on the itinerary of numerous foreign visitors. Some were bent on industrial espionage. Others were merchants who preferred to purchase cotton goods in Manchester direct rather than from agents overseas. Some were royal figures who probably had no more than a ceremonial interest, although one suspects that for many foreign leaders the sight of Manchester must have been a formative experience. One wonders, for example, what effect Manchester had on the thinking of the Viceroy of Egypt, with infant cotton manufacture in that country, who visited the city in 1846. And one would like to know what impression it made on the Grand Duke Constantine, second son of the Tsar, who came in 1847 when Russia was finding herself increasingly backward in economic development. The answers await further investigation.

The most detailed reactions came from foreigners exploring what was often termed 'the social question' – that more general version of what in Britain had been termed 'the condition of England question'. Everywhere in western Europe, thoughtful observers were frightened and puzzled by the sudden growth in the size of the working class, particularly in cities, and the seeming deterioration in its standard of living and political loyalty. Poverty, starvation, disease and defiance of the State had been features of life for centuries. But they seemed to contemporaries to be more visible and more socially volatile as a result of industrialisation and the growth of cities.

Manchester prompted great interest among analysts addressing these questions. One problem frequently noted by foreign observers was the poor health of the town's workers. The French seem to have focuswd on this aspect earlier than the Germans, perhaps because of French leadership in the nerwly developing discipline of sociology and the fund of international scientific experience gained during the Napoleonic wars. As early as 1828 one French visitor, Gustav d'Eichtal, studied the heavy demands made upon the health of individuals by the cotton industry. He found many Manchester manufacturers civil and well mannered, but concluded that economic survival was reserved only for those able to withstand severe hardships of mind and body, while the same pressures were felt even more acutely by workers. By 1840 the ability of labourers in Manchester and elsewhere to withstand such strain had been made the subject of an intensive study by Louis Villermé, one of the editors of the *Annales d'Hygiène* (founded 1829), probably the first journal of public health in history. The writings of Manchester public health figures were also closely followed in France. Kay's was described to French audiences in Eugene Buret's *De la misère des classes labourieuses en Angleterre et en France* (Paris, 1840) and in Léon Faucher's *Études sur l'Angleterre* (Brussels, 1845). Both writers specifically acknowledged that he had greatly influenced the leaders of the public health movement in France.

German writers also touched upon the condition of Manchester workers. One such observer was Friedrich von Raumer, who visited Manchester in 1825, 1836 and 1841. What he saw prompted him to declare that English workers, excluding children, 'receive in proportion higher wages, and live better, than those in Germany'. But he still believed that there was too much misery among the factory population, and that child labour was its most vivid sympton. In Raumer's opinion 'the easiest labour, continued twelve hours in the day, is too much for any children'. The reality was 'a slavery for them, such as has no parallel in the history of the world'. To solve the problem he advocated free trade, arguing that the miseries of the manufacturing population ultimately were caused by the high price of food and the inability of factory owners to pay their employees a fair wage.

Foreign writers also stressed the precarious foundations upon which the life of Manchester was based. An example was Léon Faucher, a noted authority on French financial and commercial policy and editor of the prominent Parisian journal, *Le Courier Français,* who visited Manchester in 1844. After comparing it with manufacturing towns on the Continent, he noted that Manchester had been uniquely favoured by nature. Climate, topography, natural resources and a local population with 'heroic' traits had combined to produce a driving force which had dazzled all Europe. But crime, poor health, economic and political uneasiness, and a neglect of culture in the higher sense were the regrettable by-products, because Lancashire in general, and Manchester in particular, were suffering from a sickness that might soon infect all England: 'Le travail excessif, l'over-working. . . Manchester en est le symbole. . .' Faucher concluded with a reminder that Manchester should never forget its 'horoscope of ambition': 'Et monté sur le faîte, il aspire à descendre.'

In July 1835 Manchester was visited for seven days by one of the most perceptive travel writers of all time, Alexis de Tocqueville. The sight prompted what one biographer, Seymour Drescher, has called 'the most powerful description of his journey. . .' Manchester seemed to the great Frenchman almost anarchic. He commented, 'Everything in the exterior appearance of the city attests [to] the individual powers of man; nothing to the directing power of society. . . There is no trace of the slow continuous action of government.' He noted the hurriedly constructed roads in and out of town, symbols of 'the incidental activity of a population bent on gain'. He heard 'the noise of furnaces, the whistle of steam', and described the six-storey factories which 'keep air and light out of the human habitations which they dominate'. Noting 'the wealth of some' and 'the poverty of most' in the growing town, he concluded, 'From this foul drain. . . the greatest stream of human industry flows out to fertilise the whole world. From this filthy sewer pure gold flows. Here humanity attains its most complete development and its most brutish; here civilization works its miracles, and civilized man is turned back into a savage. . .'

Engels and Manchester. Of all the accounts of Manchester

dealing with 'the social question', the most important was certainly *The Condition of the Working Class in England,* by Friedrich Engels, first published in 1845, and written after a stay of twenty-one months. It is the best example Manchester has ever provided to show how the decisions of even a single person about the nature of city life can affect the lives of millions. As Asa Briggs has written, 'If Engels had lived not in Manchester but in Birmingham, his conception of 'class' and his theories of the role of class in history might have been very different. In this case Marx might have been not a communist but a currency reformer. The fact that Manchester was taken to be the symbol of the age in the 1840s and not Birmingham, which had fascinated Dr Johnson and Edmund Burke in the late eighteenth century, was of central political importance in modern world history.'

When *The Condition of the Working Class* was first published it did not immediately attract much attention. The first edition was not translated from the German and thus went almost unnoticed in France and England. In Germany the work made enough of an impression for prominent economists to feel that it demanded a reply, at least three detailed criticisms having appeared by 1848, when a reprint of the first German edition also appeared. Outside the speciality of economics, however, the work's great effects initially were by way of the communist movement. Marx himself was highly impressed by the book. Soon he was writing hundreds of queries to Engels to get factual information on the English manufacturing system. Edmund Wilson has noted, 'Perhaps the most important service that Engels performed for Marx at this period was to fill in the blank face and figure of Marx's abstract proletarian and to place him in a real house and a real factory.'

Although Engels provided Marx with facts about many other British cities, most of his information was based on Manchester. The first volume of *Das Kapital,* published in 1867, contained many favourable references to Engel's work. Particularly in the eighth and thirteenth chapters, Marx relied heavily on Engels's impressions of Manchester. The volume was even dedicated to a German revolutionary exile who, Marx noted, had died in Manchester. After Marx's death, it was Engels who helped to write the last chapters of the second volume of *Das Kapital.*

One reason for the delay of interest in Engels's work can be found in the conditions of the intellectual market place at the time. His book was in competition with hundreds of other works by French and German observers – in addition to English works or translations from one language to another – which were all telling observers about the condition of the English worker.

By the 1880s, however, there were large trade union movements in England and the United States and a large socialist party in Germany. In 1885 Engels wrote, 'My friends in Germany say that the book is important to them just now because it describes a state of things which is almost exactly reproduced at the present moment in Germany.'

An English translation finally appeared in 1887, first in the United States; it was issued in England in 1892, the same year that Engels finally managed to publish the new German edition he had projected. Increasingly also the book was being cited as a fount of communist theory. Lenin regarded it as one of the truly great works the movement had produced.

Engels was born in 1820 in the Rhineland town of Barmen, directly across the Wupper river from the growing industrial town of Elberfeld, site of the first steam-powered cotton spinning machines in Germany. Here the river became polluted by dyeworks and was bordered on both sides by textile factories and shabby housing for workers. The area of Barmen-Elberfeld had already come to be known as 'the Manchester of Germany'.

The young Friedrich had an artistic temperament and continually rebelled against his father, a stern factory owner who was concerned for the welfare of his workers but seemed abrasively paternalistic. To give the son discipline, the father sent him off to Berlin to spend a year in the Prussian Guard Artillery, but in Berlin Friedrich came under the influence of the Young Hegelians, a radical political group soon to be famous as a precursor of the communist movement. The father's next compromise was to send his son to the branch of the family firm, of Ermen & Engels, in Manchester.

In November 1842, on the way to England, the young Engels stopped in Cologne. Here he met Moses Hess, who converted him to communism, and had his first face-to-face encounter with Karl Marx, who was then editing the *Rheinische Zeitung*, the paper to which Engels had already contributed several articles.

Marx was not impressed with Engels at this first meeting, chiefly because he saw him as too credulous a disciple of the Young Hegelians, with whom he was in dispute, and sent him away with a rebuff. The meeting was crucial nonetheless. In the presence of Marx Engels was reminded that the faith he had just adopted demanded more than piety; it required intellectual rigour and a tough commitment to action as well.

The latter came sooner than the former. Immediately after reaching London in late November 1842, and even before seeing the manufacturing regions of the north, he declared that working class revolution in England was inevitable. What Engels saw upon arrival in Manchester made it easy for him to strengthen this preconceived notion. England in the early 1840s was in the midst of one of the worst periods of economic and political stress in its history. The Plug Plot riots (in which radical workers removed the plugs from steam boilers in factories which paid low wages) had occurred in August 1842. Moreover, owing to a downswing in the business cycle, many of the cotton factories stood closed or idle, their owners fearing impending bankruptcy and full-scale insurrection among unemployed workers.

Beggars were even more numerous than usual: they spilled over into the more respectable parts of town. Stories circulated daily of entire families dying from starvation. Social critics of every type were receiving great support: opponents of the New Poor Law (1834) and its workhouse system; agitators for the curbing of child employment in factories and the passage of the Ten Hours Bills; Chartists; and supporters of the Anti-Corn Law League.

When Engels gained closer acquaintance with the factory system, it merely produced a personal version of the stress he saw in society. Engels found work at his father's firm in Manchester stifling, a dull routine of ledgers, statistics, price fluctuations and mechanical office tasks. He also saw the business classes socially. He drank wine and smoked cigars with German émigrés. He even joined the businessmen in foxhunting, one of the habits they had cultivated to ape the aristocracy. Perhaps unavoidably he developed a liking for many of these pastimes which was always an embarassing contrast to the doctrines he advocated.

But his general estimate of the leaders of Manchester society may be judged by his comment on Sir John Potter, an important Liberal, free trader, and MP for Manchester: 'Potter is a frightfully big and enormously fat creature, about forty-six years of age, with red hair and whiskers; three times Mayor of Manchester, very jolly, has no brains, but a good deal of belly and backside. . . he's always been a great chaser after women (he's still a bachelor) and particularly intimate with the notorious Miss Chester (alias Polly Evans). . .' Before long Engels began a love affair with Mary Burns, one of the Irish working girls who tended a 'separator' at the family factory, and this made him particularly sensitive to conditions among the Irish.

Engels left Manchester in the autumn of 1844. He stopped in Paris for another meeting with Marx, who was so impressed this time that the two conversed for ten days. Immediately upon returning to Barmen Engels began work on his book, writing to Marx in November 1844 that he was 'buried in English newspapers and books'. During this same period he was also engaged in propagandistic work for the communists; was being hounded by the Prussian police; was involved in a frustrating love affair; and was on increasingly bad terms with his father, who had now finally reached the angry realisation that his son intended to be a revolutionary rather than pursue a business career or obtain his university degree. By March 1845, when *The Condition of the Working Class* was finally completed, Engels was finding life at home intolerable, and he soon left for Brussels to rejoin Marx.

It is ironic that the ideas which gave his work its power were in some ways very trite. His picture of one town was largely conditioned by the writings of others who had already studied it, particularly J. P. Kay, the members of the Manchester Statistical Society, parliamentary investigators, and propagandists for Chartism and the Anti-Corn Law League. Engels supplemented these sources with interesting eye-witness descriptions based on his own twenty-one months stay. And he often used details from his sources in ways that gave them more artistic power: he himself emphasised that he had learned a great deal from Thomas Carlyle and Eug!ene Sue, the French novelist of Parisian life. But the visions of Manchester he offers are quite familiar, for *The Condition of the Working Class* is merely one more instance of an account of the town governed by the metaphors of underworld and savage wilderness.

There is also a lack of novelty in Engels's analysis of the social structure of Manchester. He described the town as composed mainly of a small, exploitative upper class and a huge, exploited lower class, with hardly any mediating groups in between. But to anyone who already knew Manchester the accuracy of this description would have been overshadowed by its obviousness. The distance between masters and men was one of the town's best-known features.

Modern readers have been able to find *The Condition of the Working Class* unsatisfying in a number of ways. For example, Lewis Mumford (1961) has found Engels too hasty in advocating political violence as the solution to the problems of his day, arguing that this was to fail to see the truly revolutionary potential of more peaceful changes like sanitary reform. He has also found fault with Engels's recommendation that workers confiscate the houses of the wealthy, for this would merely have intensified the spread of slums and overlooked the fact that, in the 1840s, only a very few houses of the wealthiest met civilised standards of healthfulness.

Asa Briggs likewise has taken issue with *The Condition of the Working Class*. He asserts that Engels failed to distinguish between merchants and manufacturers, thus giving the impression that all Manchester businessmen were uncultured and concerned only about narrowly economic matters, a charge which, especially among merchants, could not have been true of a cosmopolitan city that had trading links with the whole world. Briggs also feels that Engels gives the impression that Manchester was composed of anonymous, faceless classes in impersonal conflict; he stresses that this is misleading, especially with regard to the ruling classes, whose close ties of family and friendship were only one element in the town's communal spirit.

But perhaps the strongest indictment of Engels is that compiled by W. H. Chaloner and W. O. Henderson. They argue, for example, that Engels gave 'garbled and abridged' versions of excerpts from his sources but identified them as direct quotations; that he used documents indiscriminately, giving no indication of their relative accuracy or authority; that he sometimes embroidered factually accurate accounts with 'events' of his own invention; that his artist's eye and his propagandistic zeal made him seize upon the lurid, representing it falsely as the whole, and that the inaccuracy of his confident prediction of imminent revolution in Britain is symptomatic of the unreliability of his entire work.

To emphasise only the faults of Engels's work, however, is a serious distortion. Not only did it exert great force in propelling the communist movement. It also remains one of the best analyses ever written of the ways in which spatial relationships and non-verbal symbols provide keys to urban social structure. In this sense, it should be required reading for all who plan or govern industrial cities.

When Engels first mentions Manchester, he calls attention to the 'curious layout of the town'. In the centre is the commercial district, composed entirely of offices and warehouses. It is packed with traffic each day but devoid of permanent residents and 'deserted at night, when only policemen patrol its dark, narrow thoroughfares with their bull's-eye lanterns'. On the ground floor of many of these buildings are 'shops of dazzling splendour'. The commercial zone itself is surrounded by a belt of working class districts, while, beyond this belt, connected to the city centre by omnibuses, the pleasant suburban homes of the upper classes blend restfully with the surrounding countryside. It is possible, Engels notes, to travel from these restful enclaves to the commercial centre without ever being aware of the misery prevailing in the working class districts.

All the main roads out of town are lined with shops, whose lower middle class proprietors know it is in their interest to keep the fronts in impressive condition. The shops are a facade, 'hiding from the eyes of the wealthy ladies and gentlemen with strong stomachs and weak nerves the misery and squalor which are part and parcel of their own riches and luxury'. Engels says he cannot believe the commonly held opinion that this 'hypocritical town planning device', which is 'more or less common to all big cities', is merely the result of haphazard development.

By now the reader is conditioned to feel he knows where to look for the real key to understanding these seemingly random observations, and, predictably, Engels embarks on a lengthy examination of the working class districts. Most of the information that follows is not new, for he relied heavily upon Kay, Gaskell, the parliamentary reports and the hundreds of other accounts of Manchester published in the 1830s and 1840s. But no one else had ever used the details more vividly. In one passage, for example, he fits all his information into a frame, like an artist making a section drawing of part of a microscopic specimen, to produce a distinct scene described from a controlled, consistent point of view:

'The view from this [Ducie] bridge, which is fully concealed by a high parapet from all but the tallest mortals, is quite characteristic of the whole district. At the botton the Irk flows, or rather stagnates. It is a narrow, coal-black, stinking river full of filth and rubbish which it deposits on the more low-lying right bank. In dry weather this bank presents the spectacle of a series of the most revolting blackish-green puddles of slime from the depths of which bubbles of miasmatic gases constantly rise and create a stench which is unbearable even to those standing on the bridge forty or fifty feet above the level of the water. . . The houses on either side of the Irk are packed very closely together. . . All of them have been blackened by soot, all of them are crumbling with age and all have broken window panes and window frames. In the background there are old factory buildings which look like barracks. . .' Engels did for the class aspects of Manchester life what Kay a decade previously had done for the medical aspects. His achievement is in fact more accurately seen by comparing him to Kay. The latter had more faith in the possibility of peaceful change and in the adaptability of the established system. He judged the working classes more sternly. And he did not view radical structural change as a panacea: for him the basic problems were moral, and understandable only in Christian terms. Nevertheless, the similarities between Kay and Engels were striking. Both were raised in an environment that sensitised them to Manchester and the lower classes of industrial society: Kay in Rochdale, Engels in the Manchester of Germany. Both had travelled abroad before seeing Manchester, thus bringing to the town an international perspective. Both played upon the puritan sensibilities of their readers. Both had an earnest concern for the downtrodden, and misgivings about the upper classes in

10   The River Irwell just below the confluence with the Irk, 1854.
Photograph by James Mudd

which they themselves moved. Both had a talent for unifying dry facts by artistic means. Both were amazingly precise observers. Both were powerful social theorists, Kay today being underrated on this score, and Engels, though the greater mind, much overrated. And both fused disparate elements from many sources into a unique, socially powerful vision of city life.

For the foreseeable future, however, it seems likely that Engels's vision will continue to preoccupy the world more than the visions of other social investigators who visited Manchester during his era. One particular passage in *The Condition of the Working Class* helps to explain why. 'One day I walked with one of these middle-class gentlemen into Manchester. I spoke to him about the disgraceful unhealthy slums and drew his attention to the disgusting condition of that part of town in which the factory workers lived. I declared that I had never seen so badly built a town in my life. He listened patiently and at the corner of the street at which we parted company he remarked: 'And yet there is a great deal of money made here. Good morning, Sir.'

The struggle to understand the problems dramatised by this anecdote is a major obsession of the modern world. And, if not in England, certainly elsewhere, the social cleavages discussed by Engels have indeed led to the class war which he and Marx prophesied.

CHAPTER 5

Manchester and the free trade movement

In the late 1830s Manchester began to lead the way in proposing still another response to the problems created by the industrial revolution. The result was an organisation which brought more notice to Manchester than it was to receive by any other means in the entire nineteenth century.

The Anti-Corn Law League. In broad outlines the story of the Anti-Corn Law League is well known. The League owed its origins to the expanding business classes, who became increasingly impatient with the trade restrictions imposed upon them by a system of tariffs held over from the Napoleonic wars. This class soon adopted theoretical justifications for the repeal of tariffs that had been advocated in Adam Smith's *Wealth of Nations* (1776) and in the works of later advocates of *laissez faire* (the French phrase for 'leave things alone'). Tariff restrictions had been reduced by William Huskisson, Robert Peel and other parliamentary figures in the early nineteenth century. But pressure grew for total repeal. At first it was centred in London, where it received theoretical backing from the 'Westminster radicals', including James Mill, John Stuart Mill and other intellectuals with close contacts in journalism and the civil service. The cause was then taken up by more practical members of the business community who believed that the key cause of Britain's social and economic problems was the cost of food, bread in particular, resulting from governmentally imposed limits upon imports of cheap grain from America and eastern Europe.

If the price of bread and other staples could be lowered, businessmen reasoned, then workers could be paid lower wages yet still have enough to spend on food. Simultaneously, manufacturers would be able to lower the prices of their goods, force overseas competition to sell to Britain for less, and make a wider variety of goods available to all British consumers at a lower price. This logic proved attractive not only to merchants and manufacturers but also to a significant number of members of the lower middle and working classes who believed the claim of businessmen that their current rates of profit were needed for reinvestment and motivation and could not be reduced further to make money available for wage increases.

As the largest industrial city and the centre of Britain's most prosperous industry, Manchester was the logical home of a movement advocating free trade.

Wresting leadership of the tarriff reform movement from London, the businessmen of Manchester founded their own Anti-Corn Law Association in 1838, and then a national Anti-Corn Law League in 1839. The League quickly developed into a formidable political machine and performed what many had thought was the impossible task of engaging the landed interests in a lengthy parliamentary struggle. Richard Cobden, a calico printer who had led the town's movement for incorporation in the 1830s, and John Bright, a Quaker cotton manufacturer from nearby Rochdale, attained world fame by their leadership of the League. Eventually the Tory Prime Minister, Sir Robert Peel, was persuaded by the logic of the tariff reformers. He determined to yield to the Anti-Corn Law forces even if it should cause the fall of his government. Victory was hastened by the terrible famines of 1845 and 1846, which devastated both Ireland and England and made large portions of the public believe that the unrestricted import of food was imperative. In 1846 the corn laws were repealed by a parliamentary coalition of Whigs and Peelite Conservatives. So deep were the divisions on this issue that a major reordering of national politics followed. Protectionist Conservatives who had opposed Peel withdrew their support from him permanently and cast about for a new leader, whom they were to find first in Lord Derby and eventually in Benjamin Disraeli. Lacking broad support within his own party, Peel was no longer able to govern. In July 1846 the Whigs assumed power under Lord John Russell, and a number of Peelite Conservatives, including William

11   John Bright, an undated drawing by Frederick Sergent

John Bright

Gladstone, left the Conservative ranks.

Repeal of the corn laws in 1846 was followed by repeal of the Navigation Acts between 1849 and 1852, events which were seen by many to mark the arrival of the business classes upon the centre of the social and political stage. Simultaneously a new term entered popular usage as advocates of free trade were dubbed the 'Manchester school of economics' – a label traceable to Disraeli, who used the description 'the school of Manchester' in a parliamentary debate on tariff policy in 1848. The so-called 'era of free trade', maintained until the return of protection in the 1880s, when Britain began to fear the industrial growth of other nations, was marked by unprecedented prosperity popularly assumed to have resulted from enactment of the policies that had been advocated by the League.

By 1848, when violent revolutions were taking place in several countries of Europe, the example of the League was also regarded as proof of Britain's ability to change its ways peacefully through enlightened use of legal and political structures. In this sense the League was frequently cited as a contrast to Chartism, a more radical movement for social and economic change which had begun in Britain at about the same time. The origins of Chartism were diverse. One source of support was the London Working Men's Association (LWMA), founded in 1836 by the cabinetmaker William Lovett. A second base was the Birmingham Political Union, led by Thomas Attwood, a banker. A third centre of the movement was Leeds, where Feargus O'Connor made his newspaper, the *Northern Star,* a national voice for working class radicalism. In 1838 working men's associations from all over Britain adopted a 'People's Charter' which advocated voting rights for all men, annual elections, secret ballots, more equitable apportionment of electoral districts, abolition of property requirements for membership of the House of Commons, and payment of salaries to MPs so that poor people would be able to enter the profession of politics. Manchester was well represented among supporters of the charter, but Chartism tended to draw its leadership from cities where smaller-scale manufacturing created more cohesive groups of workers as well as middle class employers willing to share with their workers some of the techniques of political organisation.

In 1839 the Chartists pressed their demands upon Parliament

but were rejected. Working class violence followed in many areas, including towns near Manchester, but died out temporarily when many local Chartist leaders were arrested or fell into bickering among themselves. New outbreaks occurred in 1842, gaining strength from local discontent not always controlled by the Chartists, such as strikes by miners and rural labourers in districts where crops had failed. Simultaneously groups led by Feargus O'Connor began the Chartist Land League, demanding that workers be given their own farms as the first step in a national repudiation of industrial values and a return to the land. Again, however, the Chartist impact was limited. An upswing in sales of farm products was one important cause, and another was the care taken by law enforcement authorities to avoid provocation. By this time, competition from alternative outlets for discontent was also a factor. These included both trade unionism and the Anti-Corn Law League. The League, for its part, competed not only through legitimate means such as oratory and local canvassing but also by recruiting bands of Irish thugs to break up Chartists meetings.

As a result Chartism nearly died out for some years. Its last burst of strength came in 1848 under the impetus of widespread unemployment and revolutionary spirit from the Continent. A great rally was planned for Kennington Common in south London to carry a Chartist petition to Parliament, and at least 25,000 workers – some estimates say 150,000 or more – gathered for the occasion. But constables persuaded O'Connor and a few friends to carry the petition to Parliament peacefully in hansom cabs, and thereafter Chartism became a minor force, even though it existed officially for another ten years. All but one of the six points of the People's Charter were eventually enacted into law.

Cobden and Bright. The success of the anti-corn law campaign was due in no small part to two Manchester men who became, in the public mind, personal embodiments of the *laissez faire* doctrine which their city symbolised. Richard Cobden (1804-65) was a southerner by birth, one of eleven children of a yeoman farmer from Sussex. At the age of fifteen, to supplement his family's small income, he became a clerk in London at an uncle's cotton warehouse. In 1832 he took up residence in Manchester and with the help of friends began a promising career manufacturing and selling calicoes. He was never wholly successful in business, partly because of an unpractical streak and partly because his mind ranged so widely. Self-educated, he taught himself French, read history and plunged into the political life of Lancashire. In 1835 he visited the United States and in 1836-37 went for six months to Greece, Egypt and Asia Minor. Well written pamphlets on these trips, plus his eloquent advocacy of reform in Manchester's government, brought him widespread attention.

When the Anti-Corn Law League was formed in 1838 Cobden quickly made a name for himself as a brilliant electoral tactician and organiser of mass meetings. In 1841 he was elected to Parliament for Stockport. His speeches in the Commons won respect for clarity, command of fact, and earnestness. His most powerful defence of tariff reform, made on 13th March 1845, prompted conservative MPs to whisper, 'Peel must answer this.' But the Prime Minister was said to have crumpled his notes with the comment, 'Those may answer him who can.'

Cobden attained his greatest power in the years after 1845. Lord John Russell invited him to join the Cabinet, but he declined in order to attend to family affairs and to preserve time for travel to France, Spain, Italy, Germany and Russia, where he was entertained at banquets and inspired the formation of local free trade associations (see below, pp. 81-86). In 1849 he introduced the first parliamentary motion in favour of international arbitration and in 1851 a motion for the general reduction of armaments. The Crimean war (1854-56) led to a resurgence of aggressive nationalism, however, and in 1857, after introducing a motion condemning Palmerston's foreign policy, Cobden lost his seat along with Bright and many other members of the Manchester school.

Returning to Parliament in 1859, when national passions had cooled, Cobden continued to exert influence even though outside the Cabinet. With the help of Gladstone, then Chancellor of the Exchequer, he persuaded both Lord Palmerston and Lord John Russell of the value of a commercial treaty with France, concluded with the emperor Napoleon III in 1860. Palmerston offered a baronetcy or a place on the Privy Council as a reward, but Cobden declined. The gesture emphasised the combination

12   Richard Cobden in 1860. A portrait in oils by G Fagnani

of genuine modesty, self-righteousness, preference for being an outsider and distrust of feudality which marked Cobden's entire career. That his doctrine of non-intervention nevertheless continued to be influential was demonstrated in 1864, when Parliament refused to let Palmerston declare war against Prussia and Austria in the Schleswig-Holstein dispute. After many years of overwork and exhaustion Cobden died of bronchitis in 1865.

His political partner, John Bright (1811-89), was considered by many the greatest English orator of the nineteenth century, the figure who freed the language of politics from Johnsonian declamation and made the biblical, plain speech of Nonconformity the new standard. Bright was born at Rochdale, one of seven children of the owner of a small cotton spinning factory. Of Quaker extraction, and educated at a Friend's school, he was attracted to politics in 1830 by the excitement of hearing Orator Hunt, the radical hero of Peterloo, during an election in Preston. An enthusiastic fly fisherman and active member of the Rochdale Cricket Club, Bright gained experience in local politics from 1834 to 1841 by leading a successful campaign against compulsory payment of Church rates.

In 1838, eager for wider activities after trips to western Europe and the Mediterranean, he joined the anti-corn law struggle, speaking on behalf of tariff reform and, with his father, donating funds from the family firm. Cobden quickly recognised Bright's talent for oratory and saw to it that he addressed ever more important gatherings. Bright made his first nationally important speech in London in 1842, and from then on his reputation was secure. In 1843 he was elected to Parliament for a vacant seat at Durham.

Like Cobden, Bright was repudiated – burned in effigy, even – by a nationalistic electorate during the 1850s; and, like Cobden, he used the time for rest and for speaking tours of Europe. But in 1858 he returned to the House of Commons and from then on added his powerful voice to that of Cobden in the cause of international peace. Bright was not in all respects Cobden's ally, however. The two drifted apart in the 1860s over the issue of the American civil war, Bright supporting the north on moral grounds and Cobden favouring the south because he thought the Confederacy more favourable towards free trade.

Bright was also more sympathetic to the masses than Cobden. Where Cobden, the tactician, believed that bargaining among elites was the key to power, Bright became increasingly interested in the cause of electoral reform. The passions aroused at monster meetings which Bright addressed throughout Britain were an important force leading to the passage of the Reform Bill of 1867. From the late 1860s onward, Bright became a champion of land reform and Church disestablishment in Ireland. He was also less reluctant than Cobden to hold office, accepting the presidency of the Board of Trade in 1868 and being admitted at the same time to the Cabinet and the Privy Council. In the later years of his career, until his death in 1889, he became increasingly identified with Gladstone and other Liberals who argued against imperialistic intervention in Egypt, the Balkans and India.

The vision of an urban league. The many research studies dealing with the Anti-Corn Law League have rigorously examined the implications of 'Anti-Corn Law' but have not inquired after the origins of 'League'. The word was not often used in the 1830s and 1840s by mass movements, the most notable exceptions being the Chartist Land League and the Irish Land League – both agricultural movements which advocated broader distribution of land ownership. It is significant, moreover, that the movement against the tariff was first named the Anti-Corn Law Association and became the Anti-Corn Law League only in 1839 when a number of local associations based in towns decided to band together in a national organisation. The choice of the name 'League' is in many respects the key to understanding the movement's particular importance for urban history.

The struggles of the Anti-Corn Law League were partly an attempt to overcome feudal attitudes. In the 1830s and 1840s the landed interest was still regarded as dominant, and it was only with great difficulty that a manufacturer could become a Member of Parliament. Shortly after his own election to Parliament in 1841, Cobden stated, 'It is quite clear that I am looked upon as a Gothic invader,' and 'in Parliament I find that nothing seems to be considered so decided a stigma as to brand a man a millowner'. To the expanding social and economic class which bore these labels the stigma was frustrating in the extreme. The concern was different from that felt by the combination of rural and urban working class groups which supported Chartism, with its advocacy of broadened rights of voting and unionisation. The business classes were interested not so much in sheer subsistence as in finding a vision of their social role which would bring acceptance and justify action.

One strategy was simply to co-opt the imagery of the landed class. For example, one supporter of the Anti-Corn Law League wrote, '. . . trade has now a chivalry of its own: a chivalry whose stars are radiant with the more benignant lustre of justice, happiness, and religion, and whose titles will outlive the barbarous nomenclature of Charlemagne' (Henry Dunckley, 1854).

But the more frequent strategy, evident in League propaganda newspapers such as the *Anti-Corn Law Circular* (1839-41) and *The League* (1843-46), was the invention of an alternative rhetoric which guided action and provided intellectual reassurance. League supporters noticed that, in past eras, activities like theirs had almost always been connected with towns and cities, and that these towns and cities had usually found it valuable to band together for the advancement of common interests. Merchants and manufacturers emerged from their studies with a long list: the Delian League; the Athenian League; the economic and political connections of cities subordinate to Carthage; the great Phoenician cities of Tyre and Sidon; the alliances of medieval cities against feudal lords; the merchant city leagues of Renaissance Italy; the holy leagues of religious wars; Zurich, Geneva, Augsburg, and the other city-states of the Reformation; the trading cities of the Low Countries; the Rhenish League; and, most important of all, the Hanseatic League.

The next step in the thinking of the League's supporters was to reason from economic to non-economic factors, to the common features which cities possessed in addition to their concentration upon trade and industry. One was the frequency with which cities became directive centres of well organised crusades. In religious terms, the prime example was Jerusalem. Then there were the Holy Leagues of medieval religious wars – often composed mainly of cities – and the religious dynamism of the city-states of the Reformation. A second feature noticed by the business classes was the frequency with which cities became cultural centres. This seemed to occur some years after completion of the less delicate work of constructing a stable economic foundation. Here a number of examples impressed them deeply: the city states of the Italian Renaissance, and the towns of the Low Countries during the period from Van Eyck to Rembrandt. From these examples they began to speculate about their own potential for cultural leadership.

But here a discomforting question arose. The Leaguers reasoned that their own cities would be more powerful and more respectable to the degree that they developed on the same pattern as earlier cities. But they needed only to look around England, or to the struggling new manufacturing towns of the Continent, to compile a long catalogue of problems that kept them from achieving the ideal. At this point they too hastily succumbed to the temptation to seek a scapegoat.

The result, evident through all the propaganda issued by the League, was a one-sided denigration of rural life. To some extent the league simply replied to the agriculturalists in the terms of their own arguments. They demolished the elements of untruth in such notions as the happy and healthy peasantry, the conscientious nobility, the beauty of fox hunting, the political stability of rural life, and the intellectual stimulations of the countryside. In addition, they offered an opposing imagery, vividly portraying the plight of the urban poor, but colouring the portrayal to denigrate the aristocracy.

League propagandists saw the landed interest as responsible for slums, irreligion, drunkenness, poor health, crime and political unrest. Cities, they maintained, had been founded in the Middle Ages as a refuge from feudal tyranny. In the mood of the German saying, 'Stadtluft macht frei' ('City air makes one free') they argued that cities were therefore the cradles of democracy, freedom and the pure Anglo-Saxon virtues. Few managed to see the large element of rationalisation in this doctrine, or its limited appeal to the working classes. (They overlooked the tendency of earlier cities to be governed by dictatorships or oligarchies).

From the propagandists of the League thousands of examples of this type of reasoning poured forth. Typically a newspaper records a long speech by one of the League's salaried orators, W. J. Fox, at a mass meeting in Covent Garden on 28th September 1843. Fox's remarks were interrupted repeatedly by cries of 'Hear, hear', and the audience 'frequently arose *en masse,* and interrupted the speaker by the most enthusiastic cheering and waving of handkerchiefs'. One remark which aroused these emotions was Fox's assertion that the League's most important asset was 'the power of great cities, the agency of civilisation; of great towns and cities that first reared their towers as landmarks when the deluge of barbarism in the middle ages was beginning to subside – that in the civil wars of this country afforded the serf a refuge from his baronial oppressor, and gave him freedom – towns and cities that won the rudiments of representation – that formed our parliaments – that asserted the people's power of self-taxation. . .'

Then he added a note on the 'importance' the League 'assigns to towns and cities. It looks to them as the machinery by which this great question [of free trade] is to be wrought out of its final, satisfactory, and triumphant decision . . . because it is in towns and cities that the wrong most deeply exists which it is in the aim of the League in its noble efforts to redress.' His audience need only walk outside the theatre where they were sitting to see the proof of his assertions, in the 'by-places, the alleys, the garrets and cellars of this metropolis' where the 'wretched and famished inmates' of the poorer classes existed as proof of the evil effects of the corn laws. Finally he turned to attack the men who he felt profited from those laws. 'Landlords! They built not this magnificent metropolis – they covered not these forty square miles with the great mass of human dwellings that spread over them – they crowd not our ports with shipping – they filled not your city with its monuments of science and of art. . . They! Why, if they were to spend – if you could impose on them the laws which they would impose on you, and they were bound to spend in this metropolis all they received in their rents – if there were no toleration for French wines or foreign luxuries. . .' At this point emotion made the speaker even more incoherent, so that he spluttered on for several lines before drifting off to another topic.

Similar imagery appeared often in the oratory of the League's leaders. For example, in 1838, shortly before formal estab-

13   Anti-Corn Law League poster, undated, showing the heads of
Cobden, Villiers and Bright

lishment of the League, Cobden addressed the MPs who had refused to support repeal. Vehemently, Cobden declared that a new movement would soon be organised to persuade Parliament of the rightness of this crusade. 'There was no cause for despondency,' he said, 'because the house over the way refused to hear them. They were the representatives of three millions of the people – they were the evidence that the great towns had banded themselves together, and their alliance would be a Hanseatic League against the feudal Corn-Law plunderers. The castles which crowned the rocks along the Rhine, the Danube, and the Elbe, had once been the stronghold of feudal oppressors, but they had been dismantled by a League; and they now only adorned the landscape as picturesque memorials of the past, while the people below had lost all fear of plunder, and tilled their vineyards in peace.'

Similarly, in 1839, one of the League's lecturers declared, 'a formidable organisation, like an electric chain, has linked the great centres of opinion into one community of strength, and a single shock from the battery of Manchester will be simultaneously responded to from Ben Wyirs to the British channel.' To this his audience of 120 Bolton citizens responded with 'Enthusiastic cheering'.

It was this assertion of urban unity, more than any other factor, which made the anti-corn law forces appear so threatening to their opponents. Particularly during the working class riots which occurred over the years, observers marvelled at the tremendous social forces unleashed by industrialisation. Their uneasiness was reinforced most of all in 1842, when the riots, burnings, killings and full-scale military mobilisations accompanying the Plug Plot vividly dramatised the potentiality for political explosion. Modern researchers have shown that the Anti-Corn Law advocates were not the direct instigators of these outright acts of violence, even though the League intensified matters by inflammatory language, and even though it did seek to turn events to its advantage. At one time, however, most of the landed interest were convinced that the League was directly implicated. It took no great powers of analysis to view the amazing political machinery of the League as the germ of a full-fledged alternative to the State, and as an augury of the day when agriculture might be subordinate to a nationwide association of commercial and manufacturing centres. 'The Anti-Corn Law League is henceforth destined to become the arbiter of political parties,' proclaimed one of the League's papers in 1840; '. . . the Anti-Corn League is about to excite an electoral movement in opposition to the bread tax in every constituency in the kingdom,' said the same paper later in the year.

By 1844 the Lord Provost of Edinburgh, an unabashed advocate of repeal, could declare to his constituents, 'Attempts have been made to excite apprehensions of the League as an association too powerful and somewhat dangerous in the State. . .' It is revealing that the Leaguers so often felt it necessary to deny the validity of such 'attempts', for the very strength of denial suggests great suspicion among opponents. There were a number of charges, made both by working class supporters of Chartism and by landed interests: that the League was practising 'disguised republicanism' (landed interests); that it was 'not a democratic movement' (Chartists); that it *was* a 'democratic movement' (landed interests); that it was the 'conspiracy of a few', run by a small 'clique' in Manchester (all opponents); that it wanted to abolish agriculture or at least totally subordinate it to the trade and industry of the towns (landed interests).

The very manner in which the League propagandists denied these accusations often revealed just how accurate they were. In 1839, for example, one of the League's newspapers printed an anonymous article replying to the assertions of a citizen of Wolverhampton who accused the League of arguing 'That the manufacturing interest of this country is of so much more importance to its welfare than agriculture, that the latter ought and must give way to the former'. This, it said, was to attribute claims to the League which it had not made. 'We repudiate the narrow notion that the manufacturing and agricultural interests can ever be hostile to each other,' said the article reminding readers of the motto engraved on the League's membership card: 'Land and trade are twins; They wax and wane together.' So far the agricultural interests would have been reassured. The very next line, however, added, 'By the word agriculturists we mean the farmers and labourers; *the landowner, letting his land, is not an agriculturist any more than a shipowner is a sailor.'* The italics were those of the writer. From remarks like this, it was inevitable that the landed aristocracy should come to feel that the League aimed to abolish the old order and put a new, urban industrial society in its place.

The exact effects of this conviction on the part of landed interests have still to be explored. From research done so far, however, it is clear that feeling did lead to action, although the response of rural interests appears to have been feeble in terms of political organisation. The main attempt of the 'country' parties to reach the nation at large took the form of a loose association of local groups called 'Agricultural Protection Societies', or, in popular parlance, the 'Anti-League'. But the Anti-League was never able to recruit support from a large number of powerful aristocrats, and the preponderance of tenant farmers and agricultural labourers in its membership suggests that it was most important as an indication of even the common man's strong affection for the soil and his reluctance to accept the urban values which the League sought to impose. One might be tempted to ask why there was not more such political action, if the landed interests really were so frightened by the vision of an urban league. In a sense, however, this question misreads the times. The landed interests were indeed frightened, but they had not yet become accustomed to using political techniques of which the League itself was a pioneer. The aristocrats did oppose the anti-corn law forces vigorously, but such opposition tended to centre directly on the parliamentary arena, using the traditional means of back-room negotiation and the manipulation of parliamentary boroughs. The landed interests were slow to realise that such techniques were bound to be less effective after the great Reform Bill of 1832 and after the League had refined its techniques of extra-parliamentary campaigning. Nevertheless, Parliament still remained 'the decisive theatre', as Norman McCord, in his authoritative history, has noted. Although the League had attained tremendous strength in the nation at large, one suspects that the landed interests sensed a degree of irrelevance in this fact all along. As the son of a wealthy Lancashire manufacturer the Conservative Prime Minister, Sir Robert Peel, could himself provide them with an illustration of the possibilities for compromise. First he, and then enough of the other members of his party, realised that the Conservatives would have to yield partially to the demands of the new middle classes or else lose all. Thus the concessions of 1846 and of 1849-52, and the subsequent 'era of free trade' marked a victory for the League, but not a total victory. England did not become a society modelled on a Hanseatic League. One suspects that the landed interests could have predicted as much all along, because they knew that the steps between economic reform and total imposition of commercial and industrial values were by no means as few as the creators of the vision of an urban league had allowed themselves to believe.

Manchester's influence on liberalism and free trade abroad.
In many ways the most permanent legacy of the anti-corn law movement was its internationalism. Even in the 1880s, when tariff barriers were being reconstructed in response to growing competition overseas, the generation of Cobden and Bright was honoured for its vision of a world living in peaceful respect for diversity thanks to the unifying and educative power of unfettered trade. William Ewart Gladstone's stand against imperialistic expansion owed much to this tradition, which came to him through close association in Parliament with Cobden and Bright, and from the 1880s onwards through Gladstone's adviser and assistant, John Morley, who wrote a detailed biography of Richard Cobden. Later a new generation of Victorians, such as C. P. Scott, the editor of the *Manchester Guardian* (see below, pp. 187-192) kept the idea alive in political debate.

The anti-corn law movement also drew extensive foreign attention upon Manchester. This resulted from Manchester's close association in many minds with 'liberalism', the doctrine, first crystallised in the French revolution, and supported by the rising business class, which advocated opposition to the arbitrary imposition of government controls in politics and the market place. Politically, liberalism called for representative government, equality before the law, and freedom of the individual in matters of thought, speech, association and contract. Economically it called for removal of economic favouritism of the type the Anti-Corm Law League had battled against, and it urged governments to allow the businessman to pursue his own selfish interests on the grounds that society as a whole would benefit.

Political and economic liberalism in France. The Anti-Corn
Law League was both an example of and a contributor to this
European-wide movement. France showed the process most
clearly. There liberalism had been one of the great doctrines
articulated in the overthrow of the monarchy in 1789, and after
the July revolution of 1830 had been given embodiment in the
eighteen-year reign of King Louis Philippe. There was some
recognition that the importance of the middle class had
increased, and the richest of them, the *grande bourgeoisie,* were
able to share in governmental activities traditionally reserved
for the aristocracy.

It was in the movements to widen this narrow liberalism that
the example of the Anti-Corn Law League played its part. On
the political side, the League began to assume great importance
after its English triumph in Parliament in 1846. Among French
political figures such as Odilon Barrot and Lamartine, who
sought greater representation for the business and professional
classes, the victory of the Anti-Corn Law League was seen as
proof that reform could be achieved by peaceful means.
Somewhat like the Manchester merchants and manufacturers
who supported the League and opposed Chartism, those
Frenchmen shunned the popular movements then under way
to replace the monarchy of Louis Philippe with a republic or a
democracy based on universal suffrage. In July 1847, at a
château just outside Paris, the moderate reformers held the first
of many banquets, at which toasts and speeches were the main
weapons in the fight against the government. Like the campaign
of the English League, the banquet campaign did indeed gain
momentum as it proceeded, the main proof in this case being
its ability to win over writers and even some republicans to its
cause. Unlike their British counterparts, however, the moderate
reformers in France were soon defeated. The February
revolution of 1848 proved successful both for them and for more
extreme groups. After 1848 the model which Manchester had
provided was judged ineffectual.

Identification of Manchester with the cause of economic
liberalism took a slightly different course. Building on the ideas
of the eighteenth century Physiocrats, French thinkers from

1830 onwards had been advocating even greater application of the principle of *laissez faire* and a continued decrease in tariffs. After the triumph of the Anti-Corn Law League in 1846 several extra-governmental groups were formed in France to work for further reforms along the lines of those already obtained in England. Guiding the formation of these groups were Claude-Frédéric Bastiat, Léon Faucher, Joseph Garnier and Michel Chevalier. All were closely connected with governmental and journalistic circles in Paris, and all were careful students of Cobden and the economic philosophy he propounded.

Unlike the situation with political liberalism, the identification of Manchester with the cause of economic liberalism did not come to an end with the revolution of February 1848. By the 1850s Chevalier had become perhaps the most influential of Louis Napoleon's economic advisers. The closeness between monarch and free trader was due not only to Chevalier's adaptability and technical competence. It was also reinforced by Louis Napoleon's own great interest in providing French industry with unfettered conditions similar to those which he had judged to be present during his visits to Manchester and other English cities in 1839. The result was a series of personal negotiations throughout the 1850s between Louis Napoleon, Chevalier and Cobden himself.

So effective were Cobden and Chevalier in their advocacy that the emperor was finally persuaded, in spite of a strong protectionist bias at the middle and lower levels of his government, to use his monarchical prerogative as the means of bringing about the Anglo-French Treaty of Commerce in 1860. That the document is commonly known as the 'Cobden-Chevalier Treaty' is testimony to the close connection in the French mind between 'l'école de Manchester', 'Le cobdenisme' and the man who personified the activities and doctrines of 'la Ligue contre les lois des céréales'. The connection remained strong until the gradual return of protection in France and elsewhere from the late 1880s onwards. Cobden himself died in 1865, but the first Cobden Club, founded in London in 1866, was soon followed by others in practically every country in Europe. By this means the association between Manchester and the cause of economic liberalism was continued.

Political and economic liberalism in Germany. In Germany, as in France, there were close associations in many minds between Manchester and the cause of liberalism, though in this case interest in Manchester had a slightly wider focus than Cobden and the Anti-Corn Law League. Before the revolution of 1848 both political and economic liberalism was making appreciable progress in Germany, and attention to Manchester was one element in this movement. On the political side, liberalism was perhaps less of a tradition than in France or England, but it did draw upon the eighteenth century cosmopolitanism of Goethe and Schiller, upon a strong interest in western European political methods, and upon such demonstrations of *Zivilcourage* as the affirmation of political and academic freedom by the seven Göttingen professors who opposed abrogation of the constitution by the King of Hanover in 1837. In this tradition, interest in the political institutions of Manchester was an important element. Among journalists, for example, particularly in the Rhineland, the *Manchester Guardian* was widely read, highly respected and, as in the case of the famous liberal businessman and journalist David Hansemann, consciously imitated. As in France, the political methods of the Anti-Corn Law League were also the object of much attention among moderates who wanted to enlarge the basis of government support to include the new middle classes. In Germany, however, this interest was less widespread than in France, and centred much more among writers, professional people and academics, owing to the relative lack of industrialisation in central Europe. Nevertheless, fascination with the methods of the League could be very great. For example, the Prussian professor J. G. Kohl described the League's headquarters in Manchester at length in his travel writings of the 1840s and must have impressed many of his German readers.

Liberalism achieved a slight victory in April 1847, when the King of Prussia agreed to meet at Berlin in a United Diet *(Vereinigter Landtag)* of businessmen, intellectuals and a few aristocrats who had been pressing for increased application of liberal principles. And it was applied again in spring 1848, when moderate liberals achieved positions of power in several governments of Germany. In both cases liberals saw these events as proof of the effectiveness of the Anti-Corn Law League's methods. But as the Frankfurt parliament dragged on through the summer and autumn of 1848, entangled in the difficult question of German unity, disillusionment with methods derived from the English situation increased. As in France, the entrenchment of monarchy virtually brought an end to the habit of looking to Manchester as a model for successful attainment of liberal political goals.

The identification of Manchester with economic liberalism was also similar to that in France, though there were important variations. The first was in the means by which free trade came to be asserted in Germany. Unlike the French, the Germans could draw upon no extensive tradition of economic theory in defence of free trade. Even had such a tradition existed it would have had to grapple with the formidable advocate of the *Zollverein* (Customs Union), Friedrich List. The impetus for a free trade movement in Germany came from without, in the form of an Englishman, John Prince-Smith, who adopted Germany as his home only after being educated at Eton and serving as a journalist and banker's clerk in London. In the 1830s, while holding a teaching position in the small Baltic port of Elbing, Prince-Smith gradually became convinced that his friends among the German merchant community were severely hindered by the protectionist policies of the *Zollverein,* and began to express his views in German newspapers. His competence as an economic thinker was widely recognised in 1843, when the pamphlet *Über Handelsfeindseligkeit (Concerning Trade Rivalry)* established him as the leading advocate of free trade in Germany. Lest one stretch too far for connections which may not in fact exist, it is worth noting that specific references to Manchester occur only rarely in Prince-Smith's *Collected Works.* Nevertheless, his views obviously paralleled those of the Anti-Corn Law League.

The connection is perhaps best illustrated by noting the reception given to Cobden's banquet tour of Germany in 1846-47. In practically all cases the welcome he was given was the work of local free trade societies founded through the influence of John Prince-Smith. And, as in France, there was a great deal of focus on Cobden himself; passing through Dresden in July 1847, Cobden was pleasantly suprised to find a silk handkerchief with his picture and name on it displayed in a shop window.

As in France, the German advocates of economic liberalism were able to carry on their cause even after the failure of political liberalism. In the case of Prince-Smith, however, the elitist tendency in method is even clearer than that of Chevalier. Although free trade societies continued to exist in many parts of Germany in the 1850s and 1860s, they were never able to obtain mass support for their ideas. Tariff reductions – and there were many – were generally traceable to two other causes. The first was Prince-Smith's skill in manipulating powerful government officials behind closed doors. The second, especially after his death in 1874, was the political pressure felt by German statesmen as a result of the Anglo-French Commercial Treaty of 1860 and the constant competition for markets from Austria. Thus Bismark from time to time made concessions to free trade, even though he himself was a confirmed protectionist. Generally, however, Bismarck was so opposed to free traders, that he did not hesitate to sabotage their activities by unscrupulous methods. In 1881, for example, there were behind-the-scene manoeuvres by Dr Moritz Busch and Adolph Bucher, two of his trusted assistants. Bucher wrote an anonymous pamphlet on the free-trade cause, based on research done while on a two-week trip from Germany to the British Museum under an assumed name. Busch then used the pamphlet as the basis of signed public articles in the journal *Grenzboten,* entitled 'Some Characteristics of the Manchester School'. At the same time, both men were conducting a smear campaign to force an influential, respected member of the Berlin Cobden Club to resign.

Manchestertum. Certainly one element in the attitude of men like Busch, Bucher and Bismarck was an association of Manchester with economic threat to their own country. And this general association seems to be the best explanation for the origin of a term well known today among students of economic history. *Der Grosse Brockhaus,* the German equivalent of the *Oxford English Dictionary,* gives no etymology for the famous German noun *Manchestertum,* perhaps owing to the tendency for compilers of dictionaries to be more versed in literature than economics. The earliest reference to *Man-*

chestertum seems to date from 1861, when it was used by a member of the Prussian House of Deputies in a speech against the bourgeoisie, whom the speaker called the representatives of *Manchestertum,* that philosophy which would soon be forced to relinquish dominance to the increasingly powerful German workers' party. By *Manchestertum* the speaker seems to have meant all that is implied in the modern definition from *Brockhaus,* but with one additional nuance – German patriotism – which has since been lost. Apparently *Manchestertum* as originally coined was in part a term of denigration against those who jeopardised the well-being of Germany by selfish economic behaviour judged foreign to the national character. How easily the connotation could arise is shown by a remark made in 1863 by the socialist leader Ferdinand Lasalle. He described 'Manchester men' as 'those modern barbarians who hate the State – not this or that State, not this or that form of State, but the State in general'. These men, Lasalle declared, wished to 'do away with the State' and allow it only minimal powers of justice and law enforcement, so that they could 'wage war by means of joint-stock companies'. Their goal, in his view, was to be sure that 'nowhere in the universe' would there be a secure enclave from which 'resistance' could be mounted against them; 'armed with capital', they could then continue relentlessly in their quest for 'opportunities of exploitation'. It is probable that such remarks were conveniently misunderstood by many Germans who read them. As a good socialist Lasalle himself probably did not intend his words to glorify the German State as it then existed. But in most German minds the effect of such phrases was probably to reinforce a contrast between foreign, uncivilised selfishness and partiotic, orderly respect for the German State then in power. By 1882, at any rate, a large meeting in Mannheim of German free-traders felt it necessary to pass a resolution of protest against the habit of applying the term *Man-chestertum* to their thinking, on the ground that it conveyed an unpatriotic attitude which they claimed not to hold. These two usages suggest that the earliest coinings of the word, which one may guess to have occurred in the 1850s, probably conveyed a similar association of Manchester with economic threat to Germany. Even though the actual word *Manchestertum* probably was not used before 1850, economic fear of Manchester was not unknown. Perhaps the progression was from *Manchestermän-ner* to *Manchesteridee* to *Manchestertum,* the original connota-tion of nationalistic fear becoming increasingly abstract – in good German fashion – as time passed. This would seem to ex-plain the tendency, clear by the early 1900s, to link fear of Manchester with the assumption that both the city of Manches-ter and the noun *Manchestertum* possessed ethereal lives of their own. In a work of 1906, for example, a noted German professor of economics, Schulze-Gaevernitz, declared that, by their stress on individualism, both Roger Williams and the Quakers were 'direct forerunners of *Manchestertum*'; that Germany must beware 'the old siren-song of the Free-Traders'; that the Exchange in Manchester was for a good part of the nineteenth century 'the central point *[Kernpunkt]* of the British economy'; that the 'voice of world dominance' evident in the English doc-trine of free trade was 'even today still not dead in Manchester'; and that 'a haughty "Laissez-faire"' still sounded 'in all the utterings of this King [i.e. Manchester] of industry and trade'. It is ironic to see the pacifist teachings of men like Cobden and Prince-Smith completely frustrated.

CHAPTER 6

Legendary Manchester

Until 1840 industrial Manchester prompted no sustained literary response from any major English writer. The city had been portrayed in historical romances by popular writers of the 1830s, such as the best-selling author Harrison Ainsworth. Southey, Wordsworth, Cobbett and Shelley recorded their reactions. And Thomas de Quincey, author of *Confessions of an English Opium Eater* (1821) had published a few autobiographical passages describing the unpleasant childhood years he spent in Manchester before moving to London in the 1820s. But important changes in interest had to occur before any extensive literary discussion of Manchester was possible.

The first of these changes was the development of a desire among writers to focus upon the social problems which had been created by industrial life. Not until the 1840s did this desire become evident. Then occurred a transformation which can be understood either as a shift of interest from romanticism to realism or as a change in romantic emphasis from upper to lower class life. In any case, its result was the so-called 'social novel'. Inspired by parliamentary Blue books, by reports in newspapers and magazines, or simply by their own first-hand observations, writers began to deal with this new theme. The first result of the new approach was Mrs Trollope's *Michael Armstrong, the Factory Boy* (1840). From then on, fiction was seen to be a convenient and popular means of analysing social problems.

Carlyle and the mythic dimension. The other development which paved the way for sustained literary treatment of Manchester can best be described as a realisation of the mythic dimension of the industrial city. The source of this forward leap in artistic perception was the demonic genius of Thomas Carlyle. Carlyle made his first recorded trip to Manchester in 1838 to visit a relative. 'At five in the morning,' he noted, 'all was as still as sleep and darkness. At half-past five all went off like an enormous mill-race or ocean tide. Boom-m-m, far and wide. It was the mills that were all starting then, and creishy [greasy] drudges by the millions taking post there. I have heard few sounds more impressive to me in the mood I was in.'

This first of Carlyle's written reactions to Manchester was made public only later in the *London Life* by Froude – but it did set the mythic tone of descriptions published in the next few years. In 1839 he wrote, 'Hast thou heard, with sound ears, the awakening of a Manchester, on Monday morning, at half-past five by the clock; the rushing of its thousand mills, like the boom of an Atlantic tide, ten thousand times ten thousand spools and spindles all set humming there – it is perhaps, if thou knew it well, sublime as a Niagara, or more so.' Similarly, in 1843 Carlyle said that Manchester was 'every whit as wonderful, as fearful, unimaginable, as the oldest Salem or prophetic city'. In his view, 'sooty Manchester' was constructed 'upon the infinite abysses'.

It is instructive for the modern reader to imagine the impact of such descriptions upon Carlyle's contemporaries. The essays in which the passages appeared were phenomenally popular in his own day, and this fact suggests that they spoke to the deepest intellectual problems of that era. The passages on Manchester are a contrast to earlier literary treatments of the city in their focus on the newer, nineteenth century town of factories and commerce. But the mood is equally novel. Carlyle expresses the primitive and dramatic importance of industrial Manchester.

One is prompted to ask why he and his readers found this intuitive approach so appealing. The answer would seem to lie in their inability to understand Manchester by more logical means. As the modern critic Robert Stange has shown, something very much like this reaction was occurring at the time among writers who struggled to understand nineteenth century London. London was awesome chiefly for its diversity of life styles, its sprawling vastness, and its density of population; Manchester was interesting chiefly because it illustrated the consequence of industrialisation. In both cases,

14   Thomas de Quincey in 1845. A portrait in oils by J Watson-Gordon

however, artistic ways of looking at city life filled a deep need. As Stange has argued, 'the literary imagination has among its tasks that of domesticating our apprehension of the terrifying or the unknown. Literature can transform into myth, and thus make manageable to our consciousness experience we must live with, but which may appal or derange our immediate understanding.' Carlyle took the first step in this direction towards understanding Manchester.

Disraeli, Manchester and Jerusalem.   After Carlyle the way was open for a full-scale application of the methods of the social novel to a mythical interpretation of Manchester. It is ironic that the man who first performed this act of fusion was Benjamin Disraeli. One does not at first associate a profound artistic interest in Manchester with one of the most flamboyant politicians of the century, a man whose only literary output before 1840 had been hastily written novels about high society. Not even the acquaintance which Disraeli would have had with the political problems of Manchester will explain his preoccupation with the place.

As is the case with so many other British political figures, Disraeli's attitudes toward urbanisation have yet to be explored in detail. A glance through his writings, however, will show that to a suprising extent his thinking was dominated by a personal, idiosyncratic image of one particular city: Jerusalem. Disraeli had visited the holy city in 1831 and had been deeply impressed by the experience. Intense pride in his Judaic heritage – probably a reaction to the antisemitism he en-countered even though his father had baptised him a Christian – led Disraeli to postulate the mystic East in general, and Jerusalem in particular, as the source of the deepest strengths in Western culture.

Similarly, he believed that the answer to the political problems of nineteenth century England could be found in the concepts of social organisation articulated long before in the land of the Prophets: Disraeli's involvement with 'Young England', his desire for a more 'organic' society, his call for a return to true conservatism, and his efforts to establish a more enlightened form of aristocratic feudalism were in large part calls for an updated version of the patriarchal society of the ancient Middle East. This conviction explains many of the most characteristic features of his writings: his love of bright colours and luxurious interiors; his fascination with peacocks and elaborate gardens; his sketches of exotic personalities; his veneration for religious ritual; and, not least, his intense interest in urban life. The works of Disraeli abound in references to cities: affectionate descriptions of London streets, clubs and salons; vignettes taken from the passing city scene; sudden remarks about the great cities of other eras and other civilisations; frequent allusions to Venice and other Renaissance city-states; meditations upon the greatness of Rome and Athens; journeys to the mysterious cities of the East.

By October 1843, when he first travelled to Manchester and joined Richard Cobden and Charles Dickens in speaking at the Athenaeum, the city was vividly in his mind. His first impressions appear to have been highly favourable. His speeches freely acknowledged the greatness of Manchester. But his literary interest in the town was to take a different direction. Gradually he became more interested in the darker side of Manchester life. The first signs of this change were evident in *Coningsby* (1844), where he specifically mentioned Manchester by name, criticising it in muted but trechant manner. His sketch of Oswald Millbank, the model factory owner, symbolised the positive potential for improvement in Manchester life. His vigour, pride and contempt for the decaying country aristocracy were seen as refreshing traits, his skilful direction of his factory as indicative of a new sort of economic and mechanical genius which would benefit all England.

Disraeli made it clear, however, that Millbank was an exceptional and not a typical Manchester manufacturer. Similarly, when one of Disraeli's characters says, 'Rightly understood, Manchester is as great a human exploit as Athens,' the fact that Athenian culture had been built upon the back of a slave society was at least implied. And when Disraeli chose to begin Coningsby's education in the problems of the modern world by having him leave the forest and devote a few days to 'the comprehension of Manchester' the suggestion was again present that one's introduction to Manchester would not be entirely joyous.

With the publication of *Sybil* (1845) this interest in the problems posed by Manchester life reached mature form. *Sybil,* of course, is a comment on all of English society. The novel contains extended descriptions of London, of a rural agricultural town ('Marney'), and of a mining town ('Wodgate') as well as the usual assortment of country estates, plush salons and romantic ruins familiar to the readers of Disraeli's earlier novels. Nevertheless, it is clear that Manchester was very much on his mind when he wrote the book. Disraeli's great attention to working class life is partial proof of this. For once, a novel of his is not dominated by some awesome hero representing aspects of the author's personality, and the work contains a variety of scenes from all levels of society. In addition, it is known that, before writing *Sybil,* Disraeli had studied conditions in the north. He read the parliamentary report of the Children's Employment Commission (1842) and, through a friend, arranged to read the letters of Feargus O'Connor.

But the surest proof of his interest in Manchester can be seen in the long description in the middle chapters of the town called 'Mowbray', on the banks of 'the River Mowe' in the nothern industrial regions of England. To some extent Mowbray is an artistic composite. One critic has noted that a good deal of the business activity which takes place there seems 'more suited to Yorkshire or the Black Country than to the cotton districts . . .', another that the lower class inhabitants have too much 'Cockney quickness of wit' to be authentic Lancashire types. There is the confusing fact that Disraeli specifically mentions Manchester by name, leading one to identify Mowbray as some other place. Nevertheless, the parallels between Mowbray and Manchester are sufficiently numerous to leave little doubt about Disraeli's intentions.

Significantly, the very first description of the town carries with it a suggestion of something gone wrong. Early in the novel Lady Marney mentions that she will soon have to make the journey from her country estate to Mowbray Castle, the ancestral home which now lies in the heart of the recently expanded town. Mowbray is 'very grand,' says Lady Marney, 'but, like all places in the manufacturing districts, very disagreeable. You never have a clear sky. Your toilette table is covered with blacks; the deer in the park seem as if they had bathed in a lake of Indian ink; and, as for the sheep, you expect to see chimney-sweeps for the shepherds.' We learn that the town was for long a mere village near which, since Norman times, a Gothic castle had stood as the citadel from which Lord Mowbray's predecessors ruled the district. Disraeli's subsequent account of the family's more recent history closely resembles that of the Mosleys who actually governed Manchester. 'Mowbray was one of those places which, during the long war, had expanded from an almost unknown village to a large and flourishing manufacturing town; a circumstance which, as Lady Marney observed, might have somewhat deteriorated the atmosphere of the splendid castle, but which had nevertheless trebled the vast rental of its lord.'

A few pages later the reader gains his first direct introduction to Mowbray. Sybil, her father (Walter Gerard) and their close friend (Stephen Morley) go there by train so that Sybil may return to her convent in an unnamed 'suburb'. On a Saturday evening, two hours before midnight, the three travellers 'arrived at Mowbray Station, which was about a quarter of a mile from town. Labour had long ceased; a beautiful heaven, clear and serene, canopied the city of smoke and toil; in all directions rose the columns of the factories, dark and refined in the purple sky; a glittering star sometimes hovering by the crest of their tall and tapering forms.'

Bidding Sybil farewell at the convent, Gerard and Morley head for the heart of town, where they intend to pay a visit to their old friend 'Chaffing Jack', proprietor of a well known pub. Near midnight they enter the town centre. Disraeli's description unmistakeably recalls the Market Street of Manchester in the early 1840s. 'The streets were nearly empty; and, with the exception of some occasional burst of brawl or merriment from a beershop, all was still. The chief street of Mowbray, called Castle Street, after the ruins of the old baronial stronghold in its neighbourhood, was as significant of the present civilisation of this community as the haughty keep had been of its ancient dependence. The dimensions of Castle Street were not unworthy of the metropolis: it traversed a great portion of the town, and was proportionately wide; its broad pavements and its blazing gas lights indicated its modern order and prosperity; while on each side of the street rose huge warehouses, not as beautiful as the palaces of Venice, but in their way not less remarkable;

magnificent shops; and, here and there, though rarely, some ancient factory built among the fields in the infancy of Mowbray by some mill-owner not sufficiently prophetic of the future, or sufficiently confident in the energy and enterprise of his fellow citizens, to foresee that the scene of his labours would be the future eyesore of a flourishing posterity.'

By now the reader's conviction of something gone wrong has greatly increased. There are suggestions that not all aspects of life in and around Mowbray should prompt uneasiness – the convent, the opulence and ingenuity displayed in the main street. But the dominant emotion so far is subdued fear. In the next few lines, Disraeli's reasons for emphasising this mood become clear. Gerard and Morley turn off down one of the narrow streets which cross Castle Street. After winding through back lanes they arrive at 'an open portion of the town, a district where streets and squares, and even rows, disappeared, and where the tall chimneys and bulky barrack-looking buildings that rose in all directions, clustering yet isolated, announced that they were in the principal scene of the industry of Mowbray. Crossing this open ground, they gained a suburb, but one of a very different kind from that in which was situate the convent where they had parted with Sybil. This one was populous, noisy, and lighted. It was Saturday night; the streets were thronged; an infinite population kept swarming to and from the closed courts and pestilential cul-de-sacs that continually communicated with the streets by narrow archways, like the entrance of hives, so low that you were obliged to stoop for admission; while, ascending to these same streets from their dank and dismal dwellings by narrow flights of steps, the subterraneous nation of the cellars poured forth to enjoy the coolness of the summer night, and market for the day of rest. The bright and lively shops were crowded; and groups of purchasers were gathered round the stalls that, by the aid of glaring lamps and flaunting lanthorns, displayed their wares.'

By careful manipulation of environmental details, Disraeli has argued against the pathological consequences of one city's total subordination to a narrowly conceived version of the modern system of manufacture. By setting the scene at midnight, and by calling attention to the factories which sleep menacingly in the background, he reinforces the reader's feeling that he is getting a look at the dark underside of Victorian life which remains unexposed and mysterious to the casual daytime observer. The dangers of overpopulation and crowded living conditions are stressed, while the garish quality of the lighting contrasts with the sick complexions of the workers and the dark Hades from which they have emerged.

In succeeding pages the human consequences of this perverse form of urban life are more fully exposed. Pressing on towards Chaffing Jack's, Gerard and Morley meet a collection of characters reminiscent of Hogarth or Dickens: the 'jolly looking' Widow Carey, whose butcher's stall 'offered many temptations to many who could not purchase'; a 'little pale man' named John Hill, who tells the widow the latest details of the constant economic exploitation which he suffers as a worker at the cotton factory owned by 'those villains, Shuffle and Screw'; a deformed sixteen-year-old called Dandy Mick whose mother lies dying or drunk 'in a back cellar without a winder', and whose chief memory of her is the 'treacle and laudanum' she gave him as a baby 'to stop my tongue and fill my stomach'; and two 'gaily dressed girls from a nearby cotton mill, so fascinated by the excitement of city life that they have forsaken the opportunity to work in the more healthy conditions of 'Mr Trafford's' model factory a few miles out in the countryside.

Arrived at their destination, they are joined at their table by Dandy Mick and several of his friends, one of whom is called Devilsdust. Though only seventeen, Devilsdust is already an expert workman at a nearby cotton factory, and skilled enough in reading and writing to be the 'leading spirit' in the local workmen's educational association, the 'Shoddy-Court Literary and Scientific Institute'. But the most impressive aspect of his character is the mere fact of his being alive. 'Infanticide is practised as extensively and as legally in England, as it is on the banks of the Ganges,' Disraeli remarks. Then, in one of the most famous passages of the novel, he describes the upbringing of the baby who illustrates his proposition.

'About a fortnight after his mother had introduced him into the world, she returned to her factory, and put her infant out to nurse. . . at two years of age, his mother being lost sight of . . . he was sent out in the street to 'play' in order to be run over. Even this expedient failed. . . He always got out of the way of the carts and horses, and never lost his own. They gave him no food: he foraged for himself, and shared with the dogs the garbage of the streets. . . he defied even the fatal fever which was the only inhabitant of his cellar that never quitted it. Eventually he quitted the quarter of pestilence, and after much wandering lay down near the door of a factory. . . A child wanting in the Wadding Hole, a place for the manufacture of waste and damaged cotton, the refuse of the mills, which is here worked up into counterpanes and coverlets. The nameless one was preferred to the vacant post, received even a salary, more than that, a name; for as he had none, he was christened on the spot – Devilsdust.'

Given such an upbringing, is it any wonder that Devilsdust and millions of even less fortunate workers find themselves alienated from the classes who rule them? Of the evil factory owners, Shuffle and Screw, Devilsdust says 'Their day will come. . .' And Dandy Mick echoes this mood in even more explicit terms. '"I tell you what," says Mick, with a knowing look, and a lowered tone, "the only thing, my hearties, that can save this here nation, is – a – good strike."'In the life the masses of the great cotton manufacturing town of Mowbray are forced to lead the threat of total social disaster is clearly imminent.

Disraeli provides other glimpses of life in and around Mowbray: the regimentation of the factory girls, awakened at dawn by a paid sentry who taps their window with a shepherd's crook; the plight of Philip Warner, the hand-loom weaver displaced by industrialisation; Sybil's efforts to ease the workers' pain; the frenzied torchlight meeting at which Dandy Mick is initiated into a trade union. But all these scenes merely reinforce the interpretation of Mowbray which Disraeli had already laid down. What is most interesting in these later references is the distinctly mythic solution which they propose for the problems already outlined. At first glance, one might not suspect this to be the case. A healthy contrast to the life of Mowbray would seem to lie in the model cotton factory of Mr Trafford, in the clean air and pleasant scenery of the countryside. By the admiring thoroughness with which he describes the mill and the well run village next to it Disraeli seems to be suggesting that this is the concrete alternative to the faults of Mowbray. In exchange between Morley and Gerard, however, one can see his true feelings. If all people were as enlightened as Mr Trafford, then all would be well. 'But all men will not act like Mr Trafford,' Morley says. 'It requires a sacrifice of self which cannot be expected, which is unnatural. It is not individual influence that can renovate society; it is some new principle that must reconstruct it. . .' Gerard agrees. Clearly, Disraeli feels that the solution to the problems of Mowbray involves something more than the setting up of model factories.

Exactly what he has in mind has in fact been made clear just a few scenes earlier. 'In the centre of town of Mowbray . . . there rose a building, which might vie with many of the cathedrals of our land . . . most beautiful the streaming glories of its vast orient light!' The building is Mowbray Church. For Disraeli it is the architectural clue to that 'new principle' which will bring Mowbray, and in fact all of society, its salvation. Long before manufacturing had become the main activity of the district, Mowbray Church had dominated the prospect of the town, and served as a headquarters of the surrounding parish. In more recent times industrialisation meant that 'an immense population gathered round the sacred citadel and gradually spread on all sides of it for miles'. (The parallel with the Collegiate Church of Manchester is striking). With manufacturing, however, had come an overemphasis on more wordly things. Attendance at the Church had begun to wane, and the parish was falling prey to Church politics. The task of remedying matters falls to the new vicar, Aubrey St Lys, who came to Mowbray 'among a hundred thousand heathen to preach "the unknown God"'. Only when Mowbray returns to the guiding principles of this 'unknown God', Disraeli argues, will the town solve the problems which have so grievously beset it in modern times. The doctorines which underlie such worship, however, are much more an expression of his own particular mythic vision than of anything which could be fully termed orthodox Anglicanism. At one point he engages Aubrey St Lys in a conversation on the legitimacy of Catholicism. The Church of Rome deserves respect, St Lys says, but men must not forget 'its early and apostolical character, when it was fresh from Palestine, and as it were fragrant from Paradise. . . The apostles succeeded the prophets. . . the order of our priesthood came directly from Jehovah. . . When Omnipotence deigned to be incarnate, the Ineffable Word did not select a Roman frame. The prophets were not Romans; the apostles were not Romans; she, who was blessed above all women, I never heard she was a Roman maiden. No, I should look to a land more distant than Italy, to a city more sacred even than Rome.' When Mowbray – and, by implication, Manchester – learns to look toward Jerusalem, then it will be redeemed.

Elizabeth Gaskell.   The next major literary attempts to deal with Manchester were *Mary Barton* and *North and South*. The author of these novels, Elizabeth Cleghorn Stevenson, was born in 1810 in Chelsea. That same year, shortly after her mother's death, she was taken by stagecoach to the rural village of Knutsford, sixteen miles south-west of Manchester. In 1832 she married a Unitarian minister, the Rev. William Gaskell, then junior minister at Cross Street Chapel, where he was to serve for the next fifty-two years.

Moving to Manchester was a predictable shock. Mrs Gaskell noticed, for example, that muslin curtains would not stay clean for more than a week because of the soot. She not only assisted her husband in social duties but saw the suffering of workers at first hand through such activities as calling at the homes of Sunday school pupils. She soon took to writing as an outlet for her nervous energy. She was encouraged by her husband, who possessed a considerable literary talent of his own and had become an expert on Lancashire dialects. From 1837, the date of her first published piece, her reputation grew, and by the mid 1840s she was a nationally known novelist.

Mrs Gaskell's first novel which deals with Manchester life was *Mary Barton,* published in 1848. It is the story of John Barton, an upstanding weaver, and of his loyal daughter Mary. As the novel opens, conditions in Manchester are good, and both John and his master enjoy the general prosperity. Then economic distress strikes the town, and John Barton loses his job when his master's factory closes. With no savings to see him through the difficulty, he watches in sorrow as his wife and little son die of privation. Only Mary remains. She, meanwhile, finds that two young men are romantically attracted to her: Jem Wilson, a worker of her own class, and young Mr Carson, the son of a rich factory owner. The distress of the moment soon

entangles all these figures in tragedy. Angered at the failure
of Parliament to aid the workers, John Barton becomes a
Chartist, and also takes opium to relieve his hunger. When the
Chartists discover that young Mr Carson has publicly mocked
them they secretly decide to assassinate him. For this task John
Barton is chosen by lot. Although Jem Wilson is first accused
of the murder, Mary soon comes to believe that her father has
done it. Jem is eventually cleared of suspicion, and at his trial
learns of Mary's love for him. Though John Barton is never
formally accused, he eventually finds that he can bear the
weight of his guilt no longer. After an anguished confession to
his daughter he dies of grief. The novel ends with Mary and
Jem deciding to seek a new and better life together in Canada.

The chief interest of the story lies in the opportunity it gives
Mrs Gaskell to reveal little known details of Manchester life.
As the novel opens, for example, several workers are spending
a restful afternoon in the pleasant green countryside around
about. Gradually their differences from rural people are shown,
and they begin to discuss the problems which are their lot as
dwellers in the city. As they return the reader is given long
descriptions of their homes, their customs, their hopes and fears.
In the usual manner of the social novel, the whole effect is very
like a travelogue which reveals to the middle class public the
little known features of lower class life.

In due course, the homes and attitudes of the manufacturers
are described, and the conflicts of interest between the two
groups play themselves out. As the moral downfall of John
Barton proceeds it becomes evident that Mrs Gaskell has
subordinated all the details of her story to the argument that
the way of life in Manchester forces tragedy upon fundamentally
decent people. The reader's feelings at the end of the book are
of sympathy and pessimism. The persona of the authoress is
that of a nurse who sees no final remedy for the sorrow she
witnesses daily, but who stresses the importance of bearing with
the sufferers nonetheless.

Only in the most partial way does she deal with the question
of how to find a general solution to the difficulties she so vividly
catalogues. Some hope, she suggests, can be found in escape.
Thus for Mary and Jem Wilson marriage and emigration to
Canada are the proper response to all they have endured in

Manchester. As the novel closes, they are depicted in the new-found happiness which this response has made possible, and their joy is reminiscent of the pastoral calm with which the novel opened.

Any hopes which lie in flight to a simpler society are blunted, however, by recollection of the contrasts between country and city life which Mrs Gaskell has voiced in these same early scenes. There she noted a 'deficiency of sense' in the rural inhabitants which the city dwellers did not possess. Even this single phrase is enough to show that the frequent dullness of country life was for her proof that it, too, possessed serious drawbacks. Ultimately the reader finds no panacea in mere change of environment.

We are forced to fall back on the words of one of the minor characters of the story, a wise friend of the Bartons fittingly named Job Legh. At several points in the story Job's reflections have served as a mediating influence between workers and factory owners, and it is his philosophy which seems most appropriate to the wife of a Unitarian minister. Job voices the hope that '. . . a perfect understanding, and complete confidence and love, might exist between masters and men; that the truth might be recognised that the interests of one were the interests of all; and, as such, required the consideration and deliberation of all;. . . in short, to acknowledge the Spirit of Christ as the regulating law between both parties.'

In the six years between the appearance of *Mary Barton* and the publication of her next Manchester novel Mrs Gaskell only slightly modified the outlook which Job Legh had expressed. It is true that her views had softened somewhat by the time *North and South* was published in 1854. She noted the comments of reviewers who thought *Mary Barton* contained too many death-bed scenes. She was also sensitive to the many writers – the local industrialist W. R. Greg being the most vociferous – who sided with manufacturers in calling her portrait of Manchester in *Mary Barton* grossly unfair. There was, too, a slight change in her own opinions as she came to know Manchester more intimately. She was particularly influenced by the friendship which she and her husband enjoyed with James Nasmyth, inventor of the steam hammer and one of the more kindhearted manufacturers. The acquaintance helped to soften her earlier

15 Elizabeth Gaskell, a photograph taken about 1860
16 The sitting-room in Plymouth Grove, the Gaskell's home

impulses toward pessimism. Even so, the change in her attitude was more a matter of emphasis than doctrine. As in *Mary Barton,* the themes of *North and South* were suffering and conflict. And, as in *Mary Barton,* the solution to problems lay not in a change of environment but in Christian love. In *North and South,* however, the commitment to this solution is more complex and more intense.

North and South is constructed in terms of a classic series of opposing themes in English life. The north represents rough topography, cold climate, large cities, manufacturing, religious dissent, emphasis on work, absence of cultural polish. The south is symbolised by green countryside, mild climate, picturesque villages, agriculture and ancient handicrafts, religious orthodoxy, a leisurely pace of life, and concern for the more refined aspects of civilisation. The possibility of reconciling these opposites is explored through the character of Margaret Hale, who is taken by her father from the peaceful southern village of 'Helstone' to the bustling northern town of 'Milton' in the county of 'Darkshire'. The autobiographical strain in the novel is strong, and Maragret Hale's gradual adjustment to Milton closely parallels Mrs Gaskell's own transition from Knutsford to Manchester. As in *Mary Barton,* the gradual shift from country to city also develops into an extended exploration of the life of the town, and, as in *Mary Barton,* this exploration ultimately ends in ambivalence about the relative virtues of town and country life.

'I suppose each mode of life produces its own trials and its own temptations. The dweller in towns must find it as difficult to be patient and calm, as the country-bred man must find it to be active, and equal to unwonted emergencies. Both must find it hard to realise a future of any kind: the one because the present is so living and hurrying and close around him; the other because his life tempts him to revel in the mere sense of animal existence, not knowing of, and consequently not caring for, any pungency of pleasure, for the attainment of which he can plan, and deny himself, and look forward.'

Even more explicitly than in *Mary Barton,* then, Mrs Gaskell stresses that no final solution lies in merely changing the environment. She takes this idea one step further by specifying the limited value of changes in the social and economic system.

Significantly, the character she uses to state her view is the prominent Milton manufacturer John Thornton. Unlike Mr Carson, the equivalent character in *Mary Barton,* John Thornton is noticeably humane (usually assumed to be modelled upon James Nasmyth). From the opening scenes of the novel, his northern sternness is tempered by a strong sympathy for those less fortunate than himself.

His impulses in this direction are strengthened when he suffers bankruptcy, an experience which forces him to acknowledge more completely his own fallible humanity. Sobered by misfortune, he modifies his thinking about the manufacturing system, and comes to feel that at least part of its attendant suffering could be remedied by institutional arrangements allowing closer personal contact between masters and men. He qualifies his opinions, however, by stressing that even these changes will not eliminate all conflicts. 'My utmost expectation only goes so far as this – that they may render strikes not the bitter, venemous sources of hatred they have hitherto been. A more hopeful man might imagine that a closer and more genial intercourse between classess might do away with strikes. But I am not a hopeful man.'

Neither in change of environment nor in change of system, then, does Mrs Gaskell see a solution to the difficulties with which her novel deals. Rather, she offers the same hope of an answer that she had presented in *Mary Barton.* In this case, however, Job Legh's message is formulated in terms of the central romance of the novel. As in *Mary Barton,* the heroine's gradual involvement in Manchester life includes attraction to a prominent manufacturer. This time, however, Margaret Hale can come to accept John Thornton because of his greater humanity. Thus in the later scenes the two find that they genuinely love one another. As the story has progressed Margaret has decided that she simply cannot live any longer in the stressed conditions of Milton life, and she moves first to Helstone and then to London. It is there that she and Thornton are reunited. As the novel ends, their future place of residence is left unspecified. Dominant in the reader's mind, however, is the hope which has been symbolised in their first kiss. Christian love may be enough to unite their opposing personalities no matter where they go.

Charles Dickens and Hard Times. After London and Rochester, Manchester probably played a greater role in Dicken's life than any other city. It was the home of his sister, Fanny (wife of Henry Burnett), and of his fist schoolmaster, the Rev. William Giles. The town also possessed great literary interest for him. It was a fellow novelist, Harrison Ainsworth, who first introduced him to Manchester in 1838, while in the later 1840s Dickens became a close friend of Mrs Gaskell. In residents of the area he found the models for several of his characters: the Cheeryble brothers of *Nicholas Nickleby* (William and Daniel Grant), Paul Dombey (the invalid child of his sister Fanny) and Polly Toodle (the boy's nurse). In Manchester he formed the idea of writing *A Christmas Carol,* while Lancashire served as the background for *George Silverman's Explanation.*

Equally extensive were his public connections with the city. In 1843 he presided over a fund-raising soirée for the Athenaeum. In 1852 he spoke at the opening of the first public library in Manchester (see below p. 136). There were also frequent visits to the city upon the occasion of testimonial dinners or dramatic productions of his stories. All told, he made no fewer than nineteen trips to Manchester between 1838 and 1869.

The literary culmination of this interest, of course, was *Hard Times,* published in 1854. Dickens did not form any great desire to write extensively about the industrial north until some years after Disraeli and Mrs Gaskell had put it on the literary map. Then in January 1854 he decided to treat the subject in a story for *Household Words,* the periodical which he himself had only recently founded. In addition to his desire for a sensational topic, two concerns were very much on his mind at the time. The first was working class violence. He had recently witnessed a strike in Preston, and hoped to include impressions of that experience in a story. His other concern was 'political economy'. He had recently become disturbed by popular misapplications of the principles of Malthus, Bentham, Ricardo, Adam Smith and the elder and the younger Mill. Through fiction he hoped to set the ideas of these men in better perspective. Gradually his dis-cussion of these concerns took shape. The first installment of the story appeared in April 1854. Soon, however, he faced trouble with the serial form, and found later chapters more difficult to write. Aided by critical advice from several friends – among them Mrs Gaskell – he finally completed the story in the middle of July. The last chapter of the serial was published in August 1854. In the interim the circulation of *Household Words* doubled – dramatic proof of contemporary interest which his work aroused. Subsequently *Hard Times* was published as a novel. Significantly, Dickens dedicated it to Thomas Carlyle.

Of all the major literary responses to Manchester, *Hard Times* was the most extensive attempt to understand the town by non-logical means. Dickens's means to this end was the creation of a fictional urban environment, called 'Coketown', which would prompt his audience to see mythic significance in several conspicuous features of industrial society. The weight of evidence suggests that he did not intend Coketown to resemble any one place but instead offered it as a composite based on imaginative responses to travels throughout England.

Nevertheless, both in Dickens's time and since, readers have seen Coketown as corresponding to a specific location, and one very frequent choice has been Manchester. Partly the asso-cia-tion has been the result of vigourous publicity by Mancunians anxious to justify the town as worthy of Dickens's attention. But it is also clear that Manchester was one of the places most in Dickens's mind when he wrote *Hard Times,* while Coketown itself resembles it in obvious ways. Dickens is not interested in mere realistic 'photography'. His intention is to impress on the reader selected features of the life led there, in hope that they will point the way towards subconsciously satisfying comprehension.

His most obvious means to this end is the use of symmetry. *Hard Times* begins and ends in the world of childhood. The circus is introduced early and does not return until the latest scenes. Josiah Bounderby, Thomas Gradgrind and Mrs Sparsit illustrate a trio of snobbery. Many features of the landscape of Coketown are geometrically arranged – the various 'quarters' of the town and the conspicuously rectangular buildings. Specific scenes are notable for their emphasis on geometry – the opening description of the schoolroom and, later, the arrangement of the circus acrobats in pyramids. The book is full of balanced antitheses: between the title and the more 'organic' labels ('Sowing', 'Reaping', 'Garnering') of its three sections; between the beauty of the country and the ugliness of Coketown; between the imaginative outlook of the circus and the hard-headed outlook of Coketown; the description of the railway that runs along an axis between Bounderby's country estate and the town. Sometimes this straining for regularity is unsuccessful; the attempt to attain artistic symmetry by making the marriages of Bounderby and Gradgrind simultaneous is unconvincing. Nevertheless Dickens's overall intent is clear. The reader is reassured that the urban environment is more comprehensible than he first thought; patterns can be discovered if one will simply search for them long enough.

Symmetry, however, is only one way Dickens attempts to understand the city. Far more complete are his explanations of Coketown in terms of three full-scale mythic schemes. The first is his use of classical imagery. Coketown is described as the 'Labyrinth' of the Daedalus story. The factories cast 'titanic' shadows. The inn of the novel is the 'Pegasus Arms'. Mrs Sparsit is depicted as something of a harpy, while her nose is called 'Coriolanian' and she herself is described as a 'Classical ruin'.

Throughout Dickens also hints at the mystical significance of fire. The accompanying symbolism is complex, but a major dimension and is surely its evocation of the Promethean myth. At times Dickens does recognise that the productive power of Coketown is awesome; and he admits that its competence in business and international trade is stunning. But he is also frightened by the blast furnaces of the mills. Man has stolen fire. The gods have been angered. Immense human suffering is the result. As in the case of Dickens's reliance on symmetry, these artistic relationships affect the reader mainly at a subconscious level. They allow one to refer the random details of city life to more inclusive schemes of reference with which one can feel comfortable. Though this approach may not withstand strict logical scrutiny, it conveys the conviction that Coketown is comprehensible.

The same may be said of Dickens's use of fairy-tale imagery. His ability to see life from the perspective of a child has often been noted. In portraying the life of Coketown he puts this talent to good use. The circus of the story is itself a fairy-tale world, and a reminder of the value of a childlike cultivation of the imagination. Coketown itself is anthropomorphised into an evil monster which has "jaws" and which once "terrified the Home Secretary". The factories of the town are "fairy palaces". In the mood of a beast fable, machines are compared to "elephants" and workers to ants and beetles. The tutor McChoakumchild is clearly an ogre. Similarly, Bounderby and Gradgrind are evil giants whose houses are represented as castles. The little children of the story always live in fear of being devoured by all three men, while Louisa Gradgrind is a fairy princess confined in the tower.

As one would expect, Dickens reserves his most extensive mythical references for Christian categories of interpretation. Coketown is unmistakeably reminiscent of Babylon. Factory chimneys are Towers of Babel. Coketown is assumed to be a place of sin, and its contrast to the Garden of Eden of the surrounding countryside is often stressed. Contrasts are also present within the city. Extremes of dark and light are everywhere, and a kind of Manichaean struggle is constantly taking place. The personalities who inhabit this environment are also judged in theological terms. At times this is done very specifically: for example, Rachael is a guardian angel, Sleary a holy fool, and Jeremy Harthouse "the very devil". But the attitude is more general. Failures of any character are always failures to be Christian, and redemption is a major concept of the book. Failings at the personal level are also the source of all flaws in the social system of the town. The poor, the greatest victims of this accumulation of individual sins, are portrayed with Dickensian sentimentality as particularly blessed because of their sufferings. The only solution offered for the difficulties in the systen is Christian charity. Like Mrs Gaskell, Dickens ends by saying that, until men learn to love one another, the power of Coketown can continue only at frightening human cost.

The achievement of the novelists.   Several conclusions can be drawn about the picture of Manchester evoked by the works of major literary figures. The most obvious feature of all these works is their great contrast to any rigorously factual approach, such as the statistical surveys, public health reports, parliamentary investigations, and other documents mentioned earlier in this book. In all of these documents there was a large element of subjectivity. Nevertheless, their general emphasis on a scientific approach was evident. In this emphasis, however, the novelists are deficient: their works provide only limited sociological insight, failing to convey any extensive understanding of the complexity of the urban society being discussed. Disraeli, Mrs Gaskell, and Dickens may have had such an awareness, but it was not embodied in their Manchester novels. For example, one sees no acknowledgement in their works of the contributions to public order made by improvements in local government; no exploration of the differences in outlook between merchants and manufacturers; no acknowledgment of the urban relief agencies which had appeared in the town as far back as the 1830s; no sense for the exact proportion of workers (were they even a majority?) who advocated violent responses to social problems; no information about the successes and failures of the educational institutes which workers had themselves established for their own aid; and no discussion of the possibility that at least a few of the difficulties in the newly urbanised environment might simply have been holdovers from the less urbanised ways of life of earlier eras or other places. Some of these matters, of course, remained untreated simply for lack of pages, while others probably went unmentioned because they were not sensational enough to help the novelists sell their works. One must also grant the novelists their aesthetic privileges of selection and distortion. Nevertheless, their many omissions need to be noted, because their close mingling of fantasy and selected fact could so easily be taken as the total reality of Manchester life.

Consequences also flow from the tendency to use Manchester as part of an artistic composite. Mrs Gaskell was least fond of this habit, going only so far as to give Manchester the thin mask of the name "Milton" in *North and South*. Disraeli and Dickens were more indirect. In their hands Manchester became "Mowbray" and "Coketown", and its more dramatic features were lumped with those of other English towns and then made to stand in certain ways for all of English industrial society. Not only did the actual complexity of Manchester go unnoticed; vital distinctions applicable to all of English society also remained unstressed. In a powerful but actually rather vague way, the reader thus obtained the feeling that Manchester was an archtype for all of English society. But the elements of truth and falsity in this conviction were never rigorously sorted out.

Another characteristic of all the novelists was anachronism. In *Sybil,* published in 1845, there are descriptions of wild Chartists riots and severe economic deprivation in Mowbray and the area close around it. No similar events occured on that scale in any industrial region of England, let alone Manchester, in 1845 – though they might well have occured in the course of the distresses England experienced in 1838-42. The tendency of Mrs Gaskell was similar. Although *North and South* clearly depicts the relatively calm 1850s when it was published, the story of *Mary Barton,* which appeared in 1848, is acknowledged to take place during the distresses which culminated in 1842. And in Dickens the pattern is even more obvious. Whether one assumes Coketown to be Manchester or the manufacturing regions as a whole, the extreme cultural rawness of Coketown applies more accurately to the 1840s or before than it does to the 1850s, when Dickens was even getting advice about writing from a Manchester literary figure, and when all of Lancashire was assisting Manchester in a concerted bid for cultural respectability (see below, pp. 121-130). Similarly, the extreme polarisations in Coketown between masters and men do not seem typical of any year in history after 1848, while Dickens's portrait of the menacing union agitator Slackbridge should probably correspond to an even earlier date.

One is forced to ask, therefore, why all the novelists who treated Manchester tended to look back to an earlier era. Again their desire for sensational topics comes to mind. But another explanation seems more pertinent. If fear and the desire to domesticate the unknown were uppermost in the novelists' minds, then they would probably choose the most disturbing features of Manchester life as the ones most needing to be placed in mythic perspective. The importance of chronology would become secondary, and they would search back through their memories for the scenes in Manchester life by which they had become most obsessed. Their novels would tend to become retrospective, dramatised meditations on the "time of troubles" through which industrial England – and its symbol, Manchester – had so recently passed. Although the parallel is not exact, one may recall the more recent effort of Boris Pasternak in *Dr Zhivago* to use the holy city of Moscow as a symbolic point of reference from which his characters may look back upon the struggle which their country has recently endured.

It is also important to emphasise the relative lack of interest in fictional treatments of nineteenth-century Manchester. Throughout the century, the main focus for great literature having an urban setting was always London. The features of English life that Manchester symbolised appeared somehow more susceptible to less aesthetic kinds of responses, and in the final analysis the importance of Manchester was not mainly literary. All the novels discussed here were best sellers, which suggests that the novelists knew they could rely on widespread public interest when treating Manchester in their works. But the whole development should be kept in perspective. The true importance of the novelists is that they sensed and eloquently expressed the less logical aspects of a mood – a shared curiosity which was evident along an entire spectrum of investigative responses.

PART II

The industrial metropolis

CHAPTER 7

From city to metropolis

By the year 1850, Manchester was not only a great city, but also becoming a great metropolis, the centre of a vast network of suburbs and smaller towns encompassing most of Lancashire, and parts of Cheshire and Derbyshire to the south. The population of the municipal borough, which had been 180,000 in 1838, was over 300,000 at mid-century. If one included areas immediately proximate, the figure was closer to 500,000.

The cotton manufacture continued to be the foundation of the city's prosperity, as well as of the surrounding region. There was a vigorous "home trade" and an even more profitable "export" trade. British cotton factories consumed about half of the raw cotton used by all the factories of the world. Manufactured cotton products accounted for almost half of Britain's visible exports. The Lancashire cotton manufacture, aided by its satellites in Cheshire and North Derbyshire, constituted almost three-quarters of the entire cotton manufacture of Britain. Whatever indexes one used – number of looms and spindles, number of workers or factories, cash value of goods sold – the conclusion was the same. Manchester was the centre of the most important cotton industry in the world.

The underpinnings of this prosperity were actually rather fragile. Business panics – as in 1857, for example – were part of the familiar cycle of "boom and bust" that carried over from earlier decades. There were periodic shortages of raw cotton from abroad – the most pressing being the Lancashire "cotton famine" accompanying the American civil war of 1861-1865. And, as the century progressed, British cotton manufacturers were faced with increased competition – first from the expanding cotton industries of Europe and America, and then

17 Watt's warehouse, Portland Street, photographed about 1866

from the gradual introduction of synthetic fabrics such as rayon, which required none of the geographic advantages which had made Lancashire ideal for cotton production. Nevertheless, Manchester would continue to dominate the world's cotton industry through all the decades before the First World War. So great was Manchester's economic power that, by the year 1900, some thirty-six governments had established consular or other diplomatic offices in the city.

The metropolitan region was also beginning to benefit from economic diversification. New industries spawned by the cotton industry guaranteed the city a degree of prosperity even in years when cotton manufacture itself was in difficulty. One such offshoot was the chemical industry. Manufacturers of soaps, dyes and inks expanded both their scientific knowledge and their sales to other markets. Large deposits of coal and natural gas in the Lancashire region aided these developments. For example, a number of Manchester firms were highly successful in marketing coal-tar dyes, the use of waste from local gasworks stimulated the production of sulphocyanides, carbolic acid was produced from coal-tar and a number of profitable soda factories appeared. Knowledge gained from these activities also stimulated expansions in rubber-making and the brewing industry.

By a similar process, engineering took on an economic life of its own. The mechanical sophistication necessary to run cotton machinery found application in other fields. Manchester and its region became important in the manufacture of steam engines, railway locomotives, machine tools and armaments. At the same time, the expanding cotton industries of Europe and America frequently contracted for the production of their textile machinery in Manchester.

Economic expansion on this scale brought with it profound changes in urban geography. The most basic transformation was dispersal of production facilities away from the centre of Manchester. The migration of the cotton trade showed the process most dramatically.

In the early decades of the nineteenth century, textile production facilities had migrated from the back country around Manchester, where water power was available, to locations as close to the central city as steam powered factories could be

18   Weaving shed at Howarth's Mills, Ordsall, H E Tidmarsh, 1894

located. Thus, by 1841, there were 125 cotton factories and thirty silk factories in the parish of Manchester. Proximity to the central city was desirable because it minimised time and costs of hauling raw materials and goods, and because factory offices would be closer to banks, professional services, government offices and the community. By mid-century, economic incentives were starting to work against central locations of facilities. Land prices in the central city were high. Factory and warehouse buildings were larger and needed land for expansion. Roads and canals in and out of town were improving. Railways had begun to simplify some of the problems of hauling. Most importantly, the cotton business was becoming increasingly specialised. Some factories specialised in producing one or a few kinds of yarn or cloth; or in specific parts of the production process, such as cleaning, carding, weaving or printing designs. These specialities found it advantageous to locate near one another. The result was an increasing dispersal of production sectors. For example, spinning concentrated in south Lancashire and north Cheshire. Within this area, yarns of finer count were spun in and around the town of Bolton, particularly between Bolton and Manchester, where sewing thread was manufactured. Bolton was also a centre for quilting fabrics. Oldham and certain other towns concentrated on weaving, which was centred in Northern Lancashire – Blackburn, Burnley and Preston in particular. Preston produced lighter fabrics, and Blackburn produced shirting.

With production facilities dispersed, the older, central core of Manchester remained important chiefly as a commercial centre. Here were concentrated many of the major warehouses. Here also the businessmen of surrounding areas had their offices, conducted negotiations on the Manchester Exchange, and attended meetings of such groups as the Manchester Chamber of Commerce and the Cotton Supply Association. Banks clustered in one area of the central city, newspapers and printers in another, warehouses in others. Lawyers, accountants, doctors and insurance firms each had their preferred localities and street names with which they were associated.

Here also were the various amenities of urban life which Manchester was increasingly able to support: theatres, small art galleries, concert halls, circulating and subscription libraries, political and social clubs, as well as a growing number of institutions for the working class. The two most prestigious political clubs were the exclusive Union Club and the more democratic Athenaeum. Major theatres were the Theatre Royal in Fountain Street and the Queen's in York Street. The Free Trade Hall, opened in 1853 and named to commemorate the

Anti-Corn Law struggle, was the most extensive of a number of structures available for public lectures, meetings and concerts.

At the same time, part of the social life of the city shifted to the expanding suburbs. Moving outward, the middle and upper classes purchased dwellings of sandstone in the mid Victorian 'eclectic' styles popular since the Gothic revival of the 1840s with stained glass windows, mixtures of Romanesque, Venetian and Gothic decorative elements, and small gardens at front and back. Soon, even more far-flung districts attracted the richest Manchester citizens: such areas as Upper Brook Street, Victoria Park, Rusholme, Withington, Stretford and Old Trafford. By the end of the century, large houses were being sold in Alderley, Wilmslow, Sale and Bowden.

Each time the rich vacated a district, the middle class moved outward, particularly, as the century progressed, because of horse-drawn omnibus services, increase in number of paved roads, and extension and eventual electrification of the tramway system which facilitated commuting to work.

It was necessary that this ever-growing metropolis be governed. Thus, starting in the 1840s, local government activity in Manchester expanded on many fronts. The police force was reorganised. Public health regulations required all houses to have privies with doors and coverings and an ashpit. Work was begun to improve the management of the town gasworks. Several of the old in-town markets for fish, game and vegetables were improved and reorganised. In the 1850s the municipality bought out the private companies which had been supplying water to Manchester and added additional sources of supply from the Longdendale Valley in the Pennines. In the 1870s the city council began to buy out the private companies which provided horse-drawn tramway services in the city. In 1877, after long debate, the council began the great engineering work designed to bring additional supplies of fresh water to the city from Thirlmere in the Lake District (completed in 1894).

By the end of the nineteenth century, Manchester had five 'Municipal Trading services': a gas committee, an electricity committee, a markets committee for public markets and abattoirs, a transport committee and a water committee.

The period 1850–1914 also witnessed growing prestige and

territorial authority for local government. Manchester became a 'city' in 1853, when Queen Victoria conferred this title, allowing Manchester residents to call themselves 'citizens' rather than 'townspeople' and making the town council the city council.

Further territorial growth came in 1885 when the City's boundaries were extended to include Harpurhey, Bradford and Rusholme – giving Manchester a population in 1885 of 373,000 (although the surrounding metropolitan area made the total larger).

Five years later, in response to the Local Government Act of 1888, the areas of Blackley, Moston, Crumpsall, Newton Heath, Openshaw, Kirkmanshulme and West Gorton were brought within the municipal boundary, putting the population of the City of Manchester at over 500,000. These changes were consolidated by the Local Government Act of 1894 – the last expansion of the city's territory in the nineteenth century.

By that time as well, the importance of Manchester's local government had been reinforced by the growing national representation given to the city in Parliament. The Reform Bill of 1867 had enlarged the franchise and reapportioned seats, giving Manchester three MPs and Salford two. By the Reform Act of 1884, Manchester was given six seats in Parliament, and Salford three. A. J. Balfour's term as MP for Manchester dated from this Act. In the twentieth century, another future Prime Minister, Winston Churchill, also 'stood' for Manchester.

The fact that Manchester could return such prominent conservatives to Parliament was itself a sign of major change, first exploited systematically in the late 1860s by Benjamin Disraeli's chief party organiser, the Lancashire attorney R. A. Cross. In Manchester's suburbs, where the city's new rich sought to consolidate their wealth and to imitate the ways of the aristocracy, the Tory party now found support that would scarcely have been imaginable in the great days of the Anti-Corn Law League. By the late 1880s, large numbers of Manchester workers were also being attracted to Conservatism through Tory exploitation of imperialistic nationalism and persuasive advocacy of protective tariffs as a means to increase working-class wages forced down by competition from Germany, France and the United States.

CHAPTER 8

Cultural respectability

Manchester's transition to metropolitan status was visible in a number of areas of urban life. One manifestation was growing interest in patronage of the fine arts, partly because of sincere interest resulting from more enlightened taste, but even more because this activity promised to bring social status as a patina of fashion to the expanding city. Two developments, the city's growing patronage of visual art and a similar support of fine music, show how Manchester moved awkwardly but impressively toward this coveted cultural goal.

The Art Treasures Exhibition. Public exhibitions – the famous Crystal Palace exhibition in London in 1851, for example – were a popular feature of the mid-Victorian era. They displayed not only art, but also new developments in science, technology, exploration and other fields. Influential people supported them as opportunities to display wealth and to boast of national achievements. The middle and lower classes eagerly attended to keep in step with the latest fashions, to educate themselves, and simply to be amused. Manchester had supported small scale exhibitions of art works and industrial objects ever since the 1830s. In addition, the city had always possessed a vigorous minority of artistically aware citizens. For example, the Entwistle family of Rusholme, proprietors of one of the largest cotton firms in Lancashire, frequently purchased fine paintings in Manchester. And foreign migrants, particularly Germans from Hanseatic cities and Italians, brought with them an intense interest in painting, music, tile making and stoneworking.

Manchester's Art Treasures Exhibition of 1857 drew upon

these sources but upon deeper energies as well. In a book published in 1854, Dr Gustav Waagen, Director of the Royal Gallery in Berlin, observed that the sheer bulk of great art lying unpublicised in the galleries and private estates of the United Kingdom would flabbergast anyone who took the time to catalogue it. A millenium of overseas trade, nearly a century of industrial dominance, and numerous victories in European wars had allowed the nation to accumulate a huge collection of treasures. In 1856, Waagen's remarks came to the attention of prominent Manchester citizens, including the cotton manufacturer J. C. Deane, who had been commissioner at the Dublin Exhibition of 1853, and close friends who attended the Paris Exhibition in the summer of 1855.

They noted that the Crystal Palace Exhibition of 1851, like the more recent ones in Paris and Dublin, had emphasised collections of industrial objects, but that no one had filled the gap of an art exhibition.

Deane soon obtained endorsements from the mayor, James Watts, and other businessmen interested in presenting a nationally important cultural event in Manchester. It was decided that Manchester Corporation would play no financial role in the project, though the mayor did become chairman of a council formed to gather wider support.

The first requirement for an art exhibition was a suitable building. Manchester contractors determined that one could be constructed within six months. More than 100 subscribers, including thirty-six members of the nobility of the area, guaranteed funds allowing work to begin.

By late April of 1856 those arranging the exhibition were sufficiently confident of their progress to seek Royal patronage. On 7th May 1856, Manchester's civic leaders met Prince Albert at Buckingham Palace. He told the deputation he would support their venture and asked in exchange that a share of any profits be used for the lasting benefits of the common citizens of the area. On 20th May the Queen informed the High Sheriff of Lancashire by letter that she also would attend.

The next requirement was a site. An advertising campaign was begun in Manchester papers. Writers of letters to local journals suggested numerous 'incomparable' sites, usually on the basis of economic self interest. One writer satirised this trend by suggesting Lower Broughton, because it was 'not flooded oftener than once a year, and then not much above the ankles,' and 'because I live there!'

The deciding factor was the desire to avoid the smoke nuisance. The wind at all compass directions was considered, and the question was finally decided 'nine months to three in favour of the west'. This led searchers to the cricket and racing grounds at Old Trafford, two miles south-west of the city centre along the Irwell. The executive committee noted that this was one of the few places in the city where flowers would grow.

Construction proceeded swiftly. Bricks, planks, iron pipes, girders, brackets, columns, tie rods, and huge sheets of glass began to arrive at the railway siding recently built to link Old Trafford with the main lines. Soon the outlines emerged of a vast transparent structure unmistakably reminiscent of the Crystal Palace which had housed the London exhibition of 1851.

Meanwhile the promoters worked on the organisation. Offices were rented and plushly furnished in Mosley Street, and from here the backers rigorously pressed on with the tasks of publicity and collection of exhibits. Many were obtained in the Manchester area. In September 1856, for example, *The Times* and *The Guardian* carried a small story about the Earl of Ellesmere, first president of the exhibition's guiding council, who 'while out yachting, wrote to the chairman, enumerating from recollection the following pictures, which his Lordship places at the disposal of the committee . . .' Matter-of-factly the story added that the Earl's list encompassed eleven works, including an etching by Hogarth and paintings by Jan Steen, Van Dyck and Ruysdael.

With the guarantee of a loan from the royal collection, donations of paintings from private collections became frequent. Dr Waagen's book provided the first suggestions for owners who should be approached. Eventually the backers obtained the services of George Scharf (later the first director of the National Portrait Gallery). How thoroughly he canvassed the realm for contributions may be seen from the extensive notes he took in the course of travels to collectors in all corners of England, and which are still preserved at the National Portrait Gallery in London. From September 1856, until April 1857, Scharf and his assistants achieved the remarkable record of having never asked for an unknown work of art without first giving it a personal inspection.

By the spring of 1857, with construction of the Exhibition buildings completed, the exhibits which Scharf and his assistants had collected were brought by train to Old Trafford. With the addition of passenger platforms to the railway sidings, all was ready for the grand opening. On 5th May 1857, formal inauguration of the exhibition began with a procession through the town by Prince Albert and prominent local citizens. As the Prince entered the huge glass building at Old Trafford, he must have stared with feelings of irony at the crowd of some ten to twelve thousand visitors. In 1851, in a similar situation, the artistic capital of Britain had proudly displayed the finest treasures of industry. Now the industrial capital of Britain was proudly displaying the finest treasures of art.

To many the events surrounding Prince Albert's visit saeemed to mark a new stage in the development of Manchester. *The Times* (6th May 1857) declared that Manchester was 'the scene of an event almost unique in the history of art in England or perhaps in the world'. The *Illustrated London News* (9th May 1857) wrote that Manchester now 'hurls back upon her detractors the charge that she is too deeply absorbed in the pursuit of material wealth to devote her energies to the finer arts'.

Statements like these assume added meaning if one notes the range of exhibits. The major emphasis of the exhibition was upon European paintings of the sort which would have impressed English collectors on the Grand Tour. Works by Botticelli, Raphael, Titian, Rubens, Rembrandt and Van Dyck were typical of this group. British painters, such as Gainsborough, Landseer, Constable, Turner, Millais and Holman Hunt were also extensively represented. Entire sections were devoted to British portraiture and to water colours. The exhibition also included engravings, glass and enamels, armour, fine clocks and watches, brasswork, bronzes, furniture and sculpture. All these were displayed in the various rooms against a dominant background of maroon and harmonising light green. There were about 16,000 objects, and the 1,812 paintings included in the two sections devoted to Ancient and Modern Masters alone were worth £5 million. Dr Waagen and the *National Review* both reckoned that the Art Treasures Exhibition housed at least one-third of the pictorial treasures of the realm.

On 29th June 1857, the Prince's visit was followed by the Queen's. Accompanied by the Prince Consort and members of the court, she dined with nobility in the area, knighted the mayor of Manchester, and toured the picture galleries at Old Trafford. Thanks to her visit, travel to Manchester assumed heretofore non-existent social distinction. Prominent visitors included Palmerston, Prince Louis Napoleon, the Queen of Holland, Russian nobility and the Archbishop of Canterbury. Nathaniel Hawthorne was at the exhibition one day and saw Tennyson strolling by, but did not speak because the two had never been introduced.

Middle and working-class visitors also made the trip. Manchester advertised itself as a centre of recreation, where one could see such sights as Madame Tussaud's recently opened Wax Museum near Portman Square, and where one could attend an appearance at the recently constructed Free Trade Hall (1853) of 'Professor Anderson, the Great Wizard of the North', who promised that 'Embellishments of the costliest character, apparatus perfectly novel, miracles of mechanism, and mystic means of mirth' would accompany each of his evening programmes. City guidebooks stressed the excitement of visiting ' CELEBRATED Manufactories' and in strained prose diplomatically sought to underplay the less appealing aspects of the city.

There were hundreds of special excursion trains. Employers sometimes gave workers the day off and helped to defray the cost of the rail journey. At least one Manchester manufacturer wrote his own guide to the exhibition and distributed it with tickets free to employees.

The exhibition itself featured numerous sidelights. Band concerts and performances by the orchestra under Charles Hallé were regular features. Distinguished art critics, including John Ruskin, who spoke on 'The political economy of art', were invited to give lectures. There were also lounges for rest and refreshment – one for the upper classes and a 'second class' facility for workers.

As the exhibition progressed, it inevitably received criticisms. A few seem gratuitous by modern standards. For example, one prominent Manchester minister told his audience that many of the pictures displayed at Old Trafford were 'indecent' and said he feared the dangers that would result from overlong attention to objects brought from Catholic countries. He warned that one of the Pope's 'emissaries' might be 'watching his opportunity to whisper into the ear of some lady that was wrapped in admiration of some Romish picture . . '.

Other criticisms were more serious. Connoisseurs noted gaps in the holdings of the exhibition – the poor representation of early Italian masters, for example. Many people complained that objects were displayed too closely together or too far away for easy viewing.

Minor failures aside, however, the general estimation of Manchester's venture into high culture was enthusiastic. *Blackwood's* called it a 'truly great Exhibition', and stressed that it housed 'a series of works more consecutively complete than the world has yet seen under one roof in any one city' (June 1857). The facts pointed to the same conclusion. Between the grand opening on 5th May 1857 and the time it finally closed on 17th October 1857, the Art Treasure Exhibition ran continuously for six days a week and accommodated a total of 1,336,715 paying customers, more than 3,000 each day.

None of the 16,000 art objects was ever stolen or even damaged, and order was maintained by only forty-two policemen in the day and eleven at night. The number of crimes committed at the exhibition was lower than had been the case in the Metropolis in 1851. Moreover, Manchester's was the only recent exhibition besides that of 1851 to have been financially successful – and this in spite of the disadvantages of holding such an event outside the metropolis. In a few respects, admittedly, Manchester's new 'merchant princes' failed to make their announcement of cultural 'arrival' as dazzling as it might have been. Nevertheless, their exhibition was by many standards one of the greatest in the history of the world.

A gift to Britain.   Although it was an important event, the exhibition of 1857 left no major legacy in Manchester in the visual arts. Residents continued to pursue connoisseurship individually, but the Victorian era in Manchester produced no galleries of first rank and few highly respected critics or masters of painting, drawing and sculpture. When the organising skills

19   The Art Treasures Exhibition, 1857

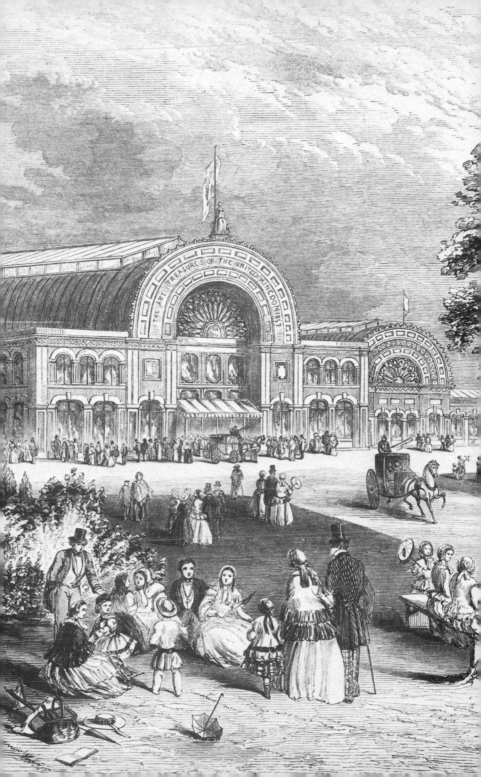

which had been demonstrated in 1857 were reassembled in 1887, on the occasion of the Queen's Jubilee, the result was a major exhibition of industrial objects, which Manchester probably would have preferred in 1857 if not pre-empted by the Crystal Palace Exhibition in 1851. The exhibition of 1887 was prestigious enough to merit the attendance of the Prince of Wales at opening ceremonies, but it was also proof that permanent, profound interest in the arts, if such was to be present in Manchester at all, would have to emerge from other currents of urban life.

Patronage of fine music proved to be the most lasting achievement of the Art Treasures Exhibition, solidifying an interchange that in fact predated the Victorian era. A regular series of Gentleman's Concerts, twelve a season, dated from the 1770s and featured music by Handel, Mozart, Haydn and Corelli. By 1839 the concerts were supported by 600 patrons at five guineas each and were performed by an orchestra of some fifty musicians. Mendelssohn conducted this orchestra in a performance of *Elijah* in 1847, although he was not impressed by the local talent.

One of the directors of the concerts, the calico printer Herman Leo, determined to improve this situation. He contacted Charles Hallé, a brilliant, twenty-nine-year-old pianist of Westphalian ancestry, whom Leo had met in Paris. Hallé had fled to London along with many other musicians during the revolution of 1848. Convinced that London could not support its surplus of musicians, Hallé was about to accept an offer for work in Bath. Leo asked him to make at least a visit to Manchester. Hallé's first experiences, unfortunately, included a recital by his dying friend Chopin at which Manchester residents demonstrated an egregious lack of feeling. Hallé later wrote that he 'seriously thought of packing up and leaving Manchester'. But Leo enticed him with the prospect that, as Hallé described it, he might 'accomplish a revolution' in Manchester's musical tastes.

Hallé appeared first as a soloist at the Gentleman's Concerts and then in 1850 became conductor whereupon he recruited new musicians, brought discipline to rehearsals, and insisted that shilling tickets be sold for the less prosperous along with the more expensive seats for the rich. In 1857 the organising committee of the Art Treasures Exhibition gave Hallé £4,515 to enlarge his orchestra and to provide daily concerts in the exhibition building at Old Trafford.

Instead of dissolving this organisation after the close of the exhibition, Hallé used the public attention which had been gained by the daily concerts to inaugurate 'at my own risk and peril', as he phrased it, a series of weekly concerts at the Free Trade Hall beginning in January 1858. The first season of thirty performances produced a profit of 2s. 6d. Eight years later the season's profit was £2,000.

The gradual upturn in the orchestra's fortunes was due not only to Hallé's ability but to the presence of energies in Manchester much deeper than those which had supported the Art Treaures Exhibition. Music touched a part of the Nonconformists soul which the visual arts, with their suggestions of image worship, sensuality and 'Popery' could never touch. Moreover, Hallé's policy of selling low-priced as well as expensive tickets catered to the democratic sympathies of the radical north of England as well as to its moneyed class.

Thus, over a period of thirty-seven years, Hallé and the Manchester citizens who backed him built one of the greatest orchestras of Europe. Hallé appeared as a soloist at almost every performance. He led the first performance in England of Berlioz's Fantastic Symphony and played symphonies by Brahms and Dvorak shortly after their first performances elsewhere. From 1876 onwards he attended the performances of Wagner's operas at Bayreuth and brought artists and interpretations from those events back to Manchester. Soloists such as Jenny Lind and Henschel came to Manchester at his urging, as did Grieg to perform his piano concerts with Hallé conducting. The Hallé Orchestra travelled to London, Edinburgh and throughout Lancashire. In 1888, Hallé was knighted for bringing the gift of great music not only to the north of England but to all of the realm. George Bernard Shaw was one of many critics who praised the orchestra for the quality of its work.

Hallé's final legacy was the Royal Manchester College of Music, opened in 1893, which he had helped to establish and of which he was principal. He died in 1895 at the age of seventy-six. The task of ensuring continuation of his orchestra then fell to concerned Manchester citizens. Three businessmen, Gustav

Behrens, Henry Simon and James Forsyth, guaranteed financial support for four seasons and immediately set out to find a new conductor. In 1899 the group was able to engage Hans Richter, principal conductor of the Vienna Opera and the Vienna Philharmonic, who led the Hallé Orchestra for the next twelve years and, in spite of an over-emphasis on German pieces, made its reputation secure. The way was thus opened for even greater successes in the twentieth century by other conductors, including Sir Thomas Beecham (1914-17), Sir Hamilton Harty (1920-33), and Sir John Barbirolli (1943-70). The Hallé is the oldest existing orchestra in England and probably the fourth oldest in the world.

CHAPTER 9

Education for an industrial metropolis

Patronage of the visual arts and music symbolised urban cultural life in the realms of aesthetics and high fashion. But Manchester had also begun, by the 1850s, to attract national attention because of its work in supporting more fundamental aspects of cultural transmission through organised education.

Elementary and secondary education. Manchester's most basic importance in this respect was its position as leader of the national movement for greater public support of elementary and secondary education. The city's prominence in these efforts had been established in the 1830s, thanks to the work of Dr James P. Kay. In 1833, the government made a grant of £20,000 for construction of schools, to be distributed through private groups. In 1836, distribution of this money was placed under a special committee of the Privy Council in education, with annual funding of £30,000. The first secretary of this Special Committee was Dr Kay, whose work in political reform and philanthropy had led to his appointment as a member of the first Poor Law Commission, created by the New Poor Law of 1834. In 1839, Kay resigned his position on the Poor Law Commission to devote full time to his growing interest in public education. Eventually he became first secretary of the new Education Department established in 1856. He was one of the major influences, as well, in the final 'settlement' of 1870, which resulted in passage of William Edward Forster's famous Elementary Education Act, which authorised creation of public school boards to serve in tandem with already existing secular and religious institutions of education.

But the respect accorded Manchester in educational circles

had other sources as well. The city could point to as fine a collection of basic institutions of education as any outside London. Manchester Grammar School, founded by Hugh Oldham, dated from 1515. Chetham's Hospital and Library had opened in 1656. Regional academies, such as that at Warrington, south-west of Manchester, had been providing a fine education to generations of children from dissenting families. In the early 1800s, the city had schools run on both the Bluecoat and Lancastrian models, the two most advanced approaches of the day, the first more Anglican in emphasis, the second favoured by dissenters. Both utilised older students as 'monitors' or 'prefects' to assist in teaching younger pupils. The Manchester Mechanics' Institute, founded in 1824, had been one of the first in England. There was a wide variety of Sunday schools. Some education was provided in line with the minimal requirements of the Factory Acts. And a number of the major national associations advocating increased public support for education had offices in Manchester. Thus, in 1870, after passage of Forster's Act, few were suprised when the first school board to be elected anywhere in England or Wales under provisions of that Act was the board in Manchester. It was generally regarded as the largest and most influential in England except for London's.

Britain's first public library.   Manchester provided equally creative leadership in the education of adult, out-of-school members of the new urban working class.

More and more workers were being taught to read and write, while improvements in printing gave them access to an ever wider range of new ideas. The middle and upper classes were both inspired and frightened by this development. An enlarged reading public might be a positive force for public enlightenment, leading to more intelligent discourse in politics, greater skills in the workplace, and increased attention to the examples of sobriety and moderation provided by the Bible and religious tracts. On the other hand, access to the printed word carried with it the potential for violent revolution, as anyone could see by reading the radical pamphlets which had accompanied every instance of mob unrest in the cities of Britain and the Continent since the French revolution. How to respond

20   Sir J P Kay-Shuttleworth (originally Dr James P Kay

to the new working-class literacy was therefore an urgent question.

One person who had thought much about the problem was William Ewart (1798-1869) a Liverpool merchant educated, like Gladstone, at Eton and Christ Church, Oxford. From 1833 onwards, Ewart represented his native city in parliament, where he softspokenly but firmly pursued a number of radical causes, including women's suffrage and abolition of the death penalty. Among major interests was the civilising potential of the 'public library' – a term just then coming into general usage. Libraries open to the general public, with no fee charged for use, were already a part of English life. Perhaps the best example was the British Museum, where, legally if not socially, all were welcome. The new term, 'public library', envisioned something more specific: a library explicitly open to all classes, and supported on a permanent basis by both national and local tax monies.

Proposals for such libraries were much in the air throughout the 1840s. William Ewart brought them to realisation. In 1849 he arranged hearings by a select committee of the House of Commons composed of MPs from major industrial districts, along with Benjamin Disraeli and the politically prominent Monckton Milnes, who showed by their presence that working-class literarcy was an issue of growing importance. Ewart led carefully selected witnesses, such as the librarian of Caius College, Cambridge, and the librarian of St Martin's in the Fields, through questions designed to buttress his own point of view. One very co-operative witness was the librarian of Chetham's College in Manchester, officially England's oldest privately endowed library open to the public. He argued that Chetham's served the professional classes well, but not the working class. Another witness was François P. Z. Guizot, the former minister of France, a refugee in England after the revolution of 1848, who was able to arouse national jealousy by describing the proliferation of public libraries in France since the Revolutionary Decree of 1791.

The report of Ewart's committee, published in late 1849, recommended that town councils be given powers to levy a small tax for new libraries. Public support for this proposal was strong, as indicated, for example, by favourable comments in *The*

Athenaeum and the *British Quarterly*. The greatest obstacle to Ewart's recommendation was Antonio Panizzi, a rising star on the staff of the British Museum (later to be the museum's principal librarian) and a powerful figure in the London art world, and yet another refugee from the revolutions of 1848. London dinner parties were set astir as, amidst expensive cuisine and tinkling crystal glasses, Panizzi and his friends spread well placed doubts about the accuracy of Ewart's evidence and the possible consequences of increased power for the masses. Panizzi reinforced his argument through letters to prominent journals. His motives were varied. He was ambivalent toward the idea of working-class education. He believed that tax support for libraries would be better used in pursuit of traditional activities such as acquisition of statues and paintings and purchase of manuscripts. And he was jealous of the parliamentary and cultural notice being gained by Edward Edwards, a self-educated Londoner of working-class background, intensely disliked by Panizzi, who had joined the British Museum staff and become chief adviser to Ewart and many of the northern businessmen who were pressing for rate-supported local libraries. Panizzi and his friends were able to spread so much doubt about Ewart's proposal that Ewart was forced to agree to appointment of a second committee and further hearings.

Finally, however, the weight of Ewart's evidence won the day. In July of 1849 his bill was passed by the House. Only a few voices were seriously against it, perhaps the most significant being John Bright, who said he supported the idea of free libraries in principle but objected to town councils being given the power to levy taxes for museums and libraries without polling ratepayers. Ewart wrote the bill to accommodate Bright's concerns.

After being approved without amendment by the House of Lords, Ewart's bill received the royal assent in 1850. Norwich adopted the Act in that same year. Winchester followed in 1851; Bolton, Oxford and Manchester in 1852. In the same year Liverpool and Brighton resolved to establish free libraries through authority already provided by local acts.

Although Manchester was not the first city to adopt Ewart's Act, it was the first to produce tangible results. Early in 1852

John Potter (later Sir John Potter), then mayor of Manchester, organised several unofficial subscription drives. Simultaneously, work began to refurbish the chosen site of Manchester's new library, the Hall of Science building in Campfield near the centre of the city, and to purchase the first books. In late 1852 a poll of ratepayers resulted in 3,962 for establishment of a Library and forty against out of an electorate of 12,500.

The Library was officially opened on 2nd September 1852. Three days before, Prince Albert had sent to Potter by railway a gift of eighteen volumes with a letter from his personal secretary conveying regrets at not being able to attend and asking that the books be 'freely accessible to persons of all classes without distinction'. The opening ceremony did not lack prestigious participants, however. Joining local political figures on the speakers' platform were John Bright, Charles Knight the publisher, the Earl of Shaftesbury, Monckton Milnes, and three literary dignitaries: Charles Dickens, William Makepeace Thackeray and Sir Edward L. Bulwer Lytton. The presence of such figures was unmistakable proof of the national importance attached to Manchester's initiative.

Dickens presented the official resolution expressing the wish that the Library 'will prove a source of pleasure and improvement in the cottages, the garrets, and the cellars of the poorest of our people'. Then, amidst laughter from listeners, he confessed that he had long wanted to know what the phrase 'the Manchester School' might mean. Some had told him it was 'all cant' and others that it was 'all cotton'. But, he explained, 'Now I have solved this difficulty by finding here to-day that the Manchester School is a great free school bent on carrying instruction to the poorest hearths'.

Lord Lytton spoke next and emphasised the chivalric theme. He was confident that libraries such as Manchester's would replace 'the old English excitements of the ale house and the gin palace'. A library, he explained, might almost be called 'a mighty arsenal . . . for books are weapons, whether for war or self-defence; and perhaps the principals of chivalry are as applicable to the student now as they were to the knight of old . . .'

Thackerary followed. Tired from a fast-paced speaking tour over previous weeks, and under strain because of financial

21   Campfield Public Library, 1852. Lithograph, unsigned

pressure, he experienced stage fright about three minutes into his remarks and simply sat down. He managed to request, however, that 'among the many sanitary and social reforms which every man interested in the public welfare is now anxious to push forward, the great measure of books will not be neglected; and we look to this, as much as we look to air, or as we look to light or water, for benefitting our poor'. Modestly, Thackeray added that, in the 'vast collection' which the library would boast, works such as his would 'occupy a very small space', since novels were merely 'tarts for the people; whereas history is bread, and science is bread, and historical and spiritual truth are that upon which they must be fed'.

The last of the speakers, Monckton Milnes, emphasised the political theme: 'It is only, remember, what lies in these books that makes all the difference between the wildest socialism that ever passed into the mind of a man in this hall, and the deductions and careful processes of the mind of the student who will . . . learn humility seeing what others have taught before him . . .'

The inaugural ceremony included an evening portion attended primarily by workers. They themselves did not speak: ironic proof that class estrangement and paternalism were still facts of Manchester life. Nevertheless, the secretary of a Working Men's Committee was able to report that some 22,000 factory operatives, clerks and members of friendly societies had raised £800 toward the cost of the new Library.

Thackeray might have used the opportunity of the evening meeting to clarify his earlier remarks, but he was still too nervous to do more than ramble on about the French novelist Eugene Sue. His point seemed to be that, in selecting their reading, honest workmen should never let themselves be misled by titillating stories of Parisian life.

John Bright also spoke. Alluding to Manchester's reputation as a 'mine' ready to explode because of social unrest, he recalled that, 'twenty or thirty years ago, it was the custom to ask at Court, if anybody came from the North of England, 'whether everything was quiet at Manchester'. Why, everything is quiet in Manchester except the shuttles and the spindles, and the forges, and the minds of the people. There is no rest here for them. Allusion was made this morning to the teaching of this new 'Manchester School.' Well, let us teach.'

Four days later, on 6th September 1852, the Free Library was opened to the public. Over the next twelve months, according to the library's statistics, its 25,000 volumes were used approximately 138,000 times. In other words, each volume was used about five times. (Manchester's population at that time was 308,000, about 50-60,000 of whom were able to read).

The crucial test of Manchester's belief in the importance of free libraries came quickly. Misunderstandings developed between the Library Board and the first librarian, Edward Edwards. In 1858 Edwards was pressed to resign and left Manchester with a face-saving announcement. To underline its commitment to working-class readers, the library board chose as successor Robert Wilson Smiles, former secretary of the Lancashire Public Schools Association (brother of Samuel Smiles, the popular author of books on self-improvement). Soon the library added many suburban branches, acquired additional volumes, and developed links with other cultural and scientific organisations. Today, thanks to this nineteenth-century foundation, Manchester possesses one of the most extensive library systems in Britain.

At the end of the century, Manchester's older tradition of privately endowing libraries was also given new life with the opening of the John Rylands Library (1899). Established by the widow of a wealthy cotton manufacturer, the Rylands quickly became one of the world's major repositories of medieval and renaissance materials. It also included many collections of importance for local history, such as the papers of Elizabeth Gaskell. The expensive, neo-Gothic design of the Rylands was architecturally stunning, but ostentatious as well, and therefore too intimidating to lend credence to the donor's claim that the collection was open to all. Nevertheless, a common theme of public munificence united Chetham's Library, the City's Free Library system and the John Rylands. To the founders, supporters, and users of all these institutions, a Manchester without broad access to books was inconceivable.

The movement for university expansion. Manchester's greatest national impact in the sphere of education was in higher learning. In this, as in many other cases, the city's combination of aggressiveness and substantial achievement – offensive to some, inspiring to others – made it the prod for developments affecting all of Britain.

Twentieth-century Britain enjoys the benefits of an extensive network of urban universities which contribute to higher learning internationally, but which are also consciously dedicated by elaborate oral and written traditions to enchancing the life of the cities they serve and to drawing upon urban energies for inspiration and fresh approaches to knowledge. Present-day citizens of the United Kingdon tend to take this situation for granted, particularly since Britain is only one of several European nations with an abundance of such city-based institutions. But specifically urban universities are not a dominant feature of all modern industrial societies. In the United States, for example, they have been rather exceptional, because many campuses in the USA were based on the medieval ideal of Oxford and Cambridge (assumed by Americans to be rural in origin and philosophy), while other campuses which appear to be urban, such as Harvard and Berkeley, were in rural or suburban locations at their founding and have adjusted to metropolitan engulfment tardily and with ambivalence.

The urban orientation of Britain's university system, and the large role which Victorian Manchester played in bringing it about, is therefore of international historical significance.

In the early nineteenth century, England really possessed only three universities: Oxford, Cambridge and the University of London – the latter founded in 1825 to accommodate a variety of groups, particularly Dissenters, who were prohibited by law from attending the ancient universities. Officially, there was a fourth university at Durham, originally founded by Oliver Cromwell to serve the north of England, abolished during the Restoration, and re-established with limited financial support in 1833 to pacify the clergy. But this institution served only a small number of students in theology and medicine and was regarded as a university only in the honorific sense.

As late as the 1830s, a rural instead of an urban emphasis was at least conceivable as the pattern for creation of any new universities in England, since English society was still dominated by landed interests and the needs of factory cities were not yet well understood. In Birmingham, Sheffield, Leeds,

Manchester and other expanding towns, however, members of local learned societies and farsighted businessmen had already founded their own small colleges catering to Nonconformists and emphasising practical skills. And, while courses at these institutions could be counted toward credit for a degree at the University of London, provincial cities were already demanding greater local control and status. In Manchester, chiefly due to the efforts of the Statistical Society, which supported research on the subject, the prospect of establishing a local university caught the eye of a growing number of businessmen, including John Owens (1790–1845), heir to a large family fortune and owner of several Manchester firms including a furrier's warehouse and cotton spinning factories. Owens was a shy, retiring man of whom little is known. In his will of 1845, he bequeathed £100,000 to establish a college in Manchester dedicated to counteracting sectarianism in religion. Trustees of the new college were to live within fifty miles of Manchester. Attendance was restricted to males. And the college was to be open to all applicants with preference first to residents of Manchester and second to residents of Lancashire – but in all cases 'without respect to place of birth, and without distinction of rank or condition in society'.

Owens's will left it to the trustees to work out details. This they did painstakingly, particularly through attentive visits to the Scottish universities. In March 1851, the new Owens College opened its doors with three full-time professors and five part-time faculty. The College's first principal, A. J. Scott, epitomises the Liberal, Nonconformist concern of the trustees that the common people be educated, since Scott had been a close associate of F. D. Maurice in the Christian Socialist movement and the efforts that were to lead to founding of the Working Men's College in London in 1854.

The early years were difficult. By 1858, the *Manchester Guardian* had pronounced Owens College 'a mortifying failure'. But the young institution had a strong sense of purpose which was already being outlined in many public forums – as, for example, in the *North British Review* in 1855, where Manchester's position as 'the metropolis of manufactures' was seen as providing almost limitless possibilities for 'an interchange of mind – a correspondence, a recognised reci-

procity, connecting ... the scientific with the manufacturing communities'. In this and similar statements,
the College propagated and defended the view – accepted in the
twentieth century but then still radical – that there was great
need in Britain for more institutions of higher learning which
would give the sciences the same status as the liberal arts, use
the city itself as a tool of education, and simultaneously give
the city a broader view of life which only higher learning could
bestow.

Outstanding faculty helped the College to carry out this
mission. For example, Stanley Jevons, who pioneered in the
application of statistical theory to economics, taught at
Manchester from 1866 to 1876, and drew upon the work of the
Statistical Society and local business. James Bryce served on
the faculty from 1870 to 1875 while still a young scholar of legal
philosophy. His famous treatise, *American Commonwealth*
(1888) probably owes its sections on the shortcomings in
American municipal government to Bryce's years in
Manchester. Henry Enfield Roscoe, the brilliant Professor of
Chemistry, shows the College's interaction with urban life in
yet another way. Roscoe served an an early Principal of Owens
College, using his diplomatic and administrative skills to
persuade local businessmen that the institution was well
managed. Simultaneously, he helped to introduce the ideas of
the great German chemist, Justus Liebig, into the English
scientific curriculum, and he was probably the first scientist in
England to supplement his income by serving as a 'consultant'
to industry.

By the late 1860s Owens College had also become more
sophisticated in fund-raising. Manchester had tarnished its
reputation by allowing delegations to approach Disraeli while
he was prime minister in 1868 and Gladstone a year later when
he held the same office, on both occasions requesting grants of
over £100,000 based on the claim that Manchester could not
provide such resources. The callers were politely told to canvas
their own city more carefully. To almost no one's surprise,
results came quickly once the appeals to Manchester's business
community were properly organised.

By the 1870s faculty, administrators, and influential
residents judged that the time was right to seek university

22　John Owens, plaque by T Woolner, 1878
23　Henry Roscoe

status. The College therefore framed an official Memorial to the Crown. National interest was assured because the future of British university life was then a subject of wide discussion due to growing interest in science and concern that Oxford and Cambridge were mired in tradition and unable to assist the nation in its competition with other industrialising countries.

Thus, prominent figures replied to Manchester's petition almost immediately. Thomas Henry Huxley judged it important enough to write personal letters to Manchester businessmen and the faculty of Owens College. He acquiesced in theory to the idea of university status, but argued that Manchester's effort was misplaced. In his opinion, the only thing new that would come from such a change was the right to confer degrees, which Huxley said he would prefer to take away from all institutions of higher learning, Oxford and Cambridge included, because the value of degrees was social and professional only, not intellectual. In another letter to College faculty, Matthew Arnold endorsed the idea of university status for Manchester but proposed that it join several towns and cities in a Federal University for the north-west of England, with Durham and Newcastle assuming a similar role for the north-east. In a speech at Oxford in 1876, Marc Pattison argued that Owens College deserved university status since its intellectual achievements had been remarkable even with the relatively small support provided by businessmen so far.

Manchester's petition forced the nation into even more thorough discussion of the relation between cities and higher learning as major journals took up the subject. Some comments played the role simply of arousing emotions. Thus, in articles of 1877, *The Times* warned that extension of university status to Manchester would undercut the important social distinction of a degree, and the *Saturday Review* claimed, 'Anyone educated in Manchester would certainly be dull and probably vicious'. But debate took on greater significance in a number of remarkable essays by some of the best minds of the era.

One attempt to give perspective to the discussion came from Goldwin Smith, the first Regius Professor of Modern History at Oxford, who went on to serve on the history faculty of the newly founded Cornell University in the United States. In February 1877, in *Macmillan's Magazine,* Smith corresponded with

British readers as 'a colonist' and argued that his New World status helped him to see the dangers of indiscriminate creation of 'one-horse' universities in the US and Canada. Amplifying these comments in the February 1878 issue of the *Fortnightly Review*, he pleaded with British readers to see that, regardless of the side they took, Manchester had confronted them with 'a really great question', namely the means by which the 'arbiters' of industrial society would be educated. Smith hoped that this question would not be decided by 'a minister who can only spare it a few hours because his time is engrossed by the government of India, the management of the Eastern Question, and the calls of party politics in general'.

A more partisan stand came in the 12th August 1876 issue of the *Saturday Review,* which maintained that large cities distracted students from their studies, while a 'very smoky town' such as Manchester could never give a student 'that keen corporate feeling which is scarcely ever wholly absent even from men who have least cared for or appreciated Oxford and Cambridge while they were in residence'.

Of all the authors of journal articles, the most strongly opposed to establishing a university in Manchester was Robert Lowe, then MP for the University of London and perhaps best known for having led the small faction of liberals opposed to expanded voting rights granted in the Reform Bill of 1867. Lowe had been vice-president of the Committee of the Privy Council on Education from 1859 to 1864, at that time the most powerful educational office in the land. He had also served as chancellor of the exchequer under Gladstone from 1873 to 1874 and would later become home secretary in 1880.

In the *Fortnightly Review* of May 1877, Lowe granted that, under the right conditions, the number of English universities might need to be increased. But he charged that, although university status might be 'an excellent puff' for Manchester, the faculty of Owens College really wanted only to be relieved of their accountability to the University of London. But this, Lowe argued, would repeat the cycle of corruption already evident at Oxford and Cambridge, where standards had fallen scandalously low because degrees were awarded by the same persons as those who taught and examined. Lowe also doubted whether a provincial manufacturing city such as Manchester could support a university with breadth of vision. Instead, it would probably 'stoop to make its teaching a school for the learning of a particular trade, such as calico printing for instance, or put Pegasus in harness to draw the wheel of a cotton mill'.

Opposing university status for Manchester on different grounds was J. Bass Mullinger, a prominent writer on education best known for his histories of the university and town of Cambridge. In the September 1878 issue of *Fraser's Magazine* he accused Manchester of 'provincial ambition' and argued that England already possessed as many genuine universities as it could support. To add new ones would diffuse limited energies into 'rival and hostile centres' and 'enfeeble and denationalise Oxford and Cambridge'. A variation of the same position was proposed by J. G. Fitch, a prominent theorist of education who had been inspector of schools in York and special commissioner on education in the great towns, among other responsibilities. In *The Nineteenth Century* for November 1878 Fitch noted that Oxford and Cambridge were looking for 'new worlds to conquer' and had recently initiated such activities as 'missionary lectures' and classroom instruction in large towns, both for men and women. By award of a 'provincial fellowship' a teacher from the ancient universities could, Fitch proposed, be 'planted' as often as necessary in industrial cities thereby removing the need for establishment of new universities and preventing duplication of functions.

The paternalistic undercurrent in such proposals was irritating to many supporters of Manchester's petition for university status. One writer who expressed his ire was Edward A. Freeman, a prominent medieval historian of the era who was personally acquainted with many of the faculty of Owens College. He later succeeded Bishop Stubbs as Regius Professor of History at Oxford. In the March 1877 issue of *Macmillan's Magazine,* in a rejoinder to Robert Lowe, Freeman described Lowe's article as 'a brief on behalf of the University which he represents in Parliament', adding that Manchester was 'anxious to be set free' from 'the yoke of London', the 'London pretence of omniscience', and all condescending parties for whom Lowe was 'the doughty champion'.

Freeman likewise voiced impatience with the 'sect' which

believed that the universities at Oxford and Cambridge were 'founded in howling wildernesses'. To the contrary, he maintained, Oxford in the twelfth century was much like Manchester in the nineteenth, 'one of the chief towns of the kingdom', an important religious, military and commercial centre – not as important as medieval towns such as London and York, perhaps, but blessed with religious freedom just as modern Manchester was blessed with 'openness to new ventures' and 'freedom from the domination of older institutions'. Like 'Paris, Bologna, or Glasgow in older times, like Leyden, Dublin, and Berlin in later times', Freeman argued, universities have always arisen 'among the busiest haunts of men' and so a university in Manchester made good sense.

Another prominent figure of the day who favoured Manchester's proposal was the noted mathematician, William Jack, a professor at the University of Glasgow who had previously taught at Owens College. Just as Goldwin Smith was able to advance England's discussion of university education from his perspective in the United States, Jack was able to offer the views of an outsider from the vantage point of Scotland. He described Owens College as 'an institution which has quietly grown into a *de facto* university before asking to be recognised as one *de jure'*, and said he was not worried that higher learning in Manchester would become excessively materialistic. Jack pointed out that universities in Glasgow and Edinburgh had, for centuries, 'contrived to maintain a tolerably high level' and had not 'yielded more than others to the genius of bread and butter. Scotch metaphysics touch no material interests; and if the names of Reid and Adam Smith, of Dugald Stewart and Sir William Hamilton, remind us of their past glories, those of the living professors of Edinburgh and Glasgow are quite as conclusive . . .'

Perhaps the strongest support for Manchester's petition came from Thomas Bazley, MP for Manchester, who contributed an article to the August 1877 issue of *The Nineteenth Century*. He noted that the attendance figures of Owens College were 'in excess of those of a considerable proportion of the German and all of the Swiss universities', and, exclusive of the medical students, closely approached those of the University of Aberdeen. He added that the College's Engineering School was already recognised as nationally important, while its laboratory of chemistry was on the way to gaining an international reputation.

Bazley was equally concerned to add his insights to those of other writers who had characterised the city of Manchester as a proper environment for a university. He commented, 'Alexandria, I believe, ran Athens tolerably hard in one period of the history of those seats of learning; and neither in Berlin nor in Breslau have industry and commerce very fatally interfered with the progress of the arts and sciences.'

Not only Manchester, Bazley added, but the entire nation might be harmed if Parliament reacted tardily to the opportunity which Owens College was presenting: 'It is by seizing such opportunities', he wrote, 'that the intellectual and social progress of nations is promoted; what Leyden did for the Netherlands in the midst of a war, and Berlin for Prussia at the close of a great national struggle, may here be done in the piping times, while they still exist, of peace.'

In 1884, after delay and prolonged deliberation, Parliament acted upon Manchester's petition for university status. The key consideration was fear of offending other industrial cities. Pressure also came from the major British medical organisations, which feared that the scientific schools of an independent university at Manchester would gain the right to certify physicians and surgeons, causing an oversupply leading to lower wages. Parliament denied Manchester's petition in the form in which it had been presented and instead created a new 'Victoria University' with limited degree granting powers, open to women as well as men, and composed of Owens College and the slightly smaller institutions at Liverpool and Leeds.

To Mancunians this compromise was a severe disappointment. But in subsequent years the city continued to help its College mature. In fields ranging from applied scientific research to education for women to extramural education for workers, it became a respected pioneer. Major benefactions, such as those by the Whitworth family of engineers and arms manufacturers, channeled funds from the economic arena into that of intellect and the spirit, resulting in fine buildings, scholarships and additional professorial chairs. All the while the College urged enactment of its original proposal.

Victory came belatedly as part of a broad expansion of universities starting in the late nineteenth century. In 1895 the older University of Durham was given a supplementary charter allowing new activities. In 1898 the powers of the University of London were broadened. In 1900 Mason College, Birmingham, obtained a charter as Birmingham University. In 1903 Manchester and Liverpool both received their own university charters with Leeds following in 1904. By then, Britain had long since acknowledged that 'interchange of mind', that 'correspondence' and 'recognised reciprocity' between higher learning and industrial cities which Manchester had advocated half a century earlier, and which distinguishes twentieth-century Britain from a number of industrial nations elsewhere in the world.

CHAPTER 10

A new corporatism

In nearly all of the towns and cities which played major roles in the life of Victorian England, a common feature is the "town hall", a type of building as old as the Middle Ages, yet of special importance in the nineteenth century. Classified by time of construction, the earliest of the nineteenth-century structures is the neo-classic town hall of Liverpool, begun in 1749 as the Exchange and modified until 1820. The latest is the neo-gothic "town house" in Sheffield, erected between 1891 and 1896. Other structures include the town hall of Leeds, completed in 1858, and that of Northampton opened in 1864.

Each of these buildings was in one sense merely the practical consequence of urban growth, a matter-of-fact response to the need for a physical headquarters large enough to house the many offices required to direct all the activities of a growing municipal government – gasworks, waterworks, markets, parks, libraries and expanded police and firefighting services. But each structure is also a statement, in architectural vocabulary, of the "new corporatism" which found growing support in British cities in the late Victorian era. This doctrine stated that the provinces were as important as the metropolis; that sensibly run local government was both a requirement and a source of national creativity; and that a heritage of common experiences had given each of the cities which grew during the industrial revolution an intangible unity which was a source of pride and a key influence upon personal character. The "new corporatism" was seldom expressed in quite this summary form. But it was eloquently articulated in many cities through complex urban dramas which accompanied the construction and opening of each new town hall.

Manchester's first town hall had been opened in 1825. Of neo-classical design, it was a strange mixture of opulence, good taste and sheer aesthetic incompetence – and in all these ways a reflection of the Manchester of that era. The city soon outgrew this building. Manchester never showed the sophistication in local government of Birmingham, the widely acknowledged leader in this activity, where, from the 1880s onward, the Chamberlain family directed a creative expansion of municipal services and civic pride known as "the civic gospel" or, more popularly, "gas and water socialism". But Manchester was impressive in its organised, relatively speedy provision of services in a highly populated region which posed problems of unusually large scale. Borough incorporation had come to Manchester in 1838; designation as a "city" in 1853; and orderly absorption of surrounding townships in succeeding years. Growth of this kind caused more national excitement in Birmingham, but contemporaries respected Manchester for its efficiency in performing a very large number of mundane but essential tasks such as laying thousands of gas lines, opening branch libraries, and ensuring proper standards of sanitation at public abattoirs. The mismanagement which otherwise might have appeared in Manchester was easily shown by comparison to the metropolis. The municipality of London was governed only by a struggling scandal-ridden Metropolitan Board of Works, and the London County Council was not established until 1889.

Local pride and managerial considerations were combined in 1864, the year the Manchester City Council officially determined that a larger building was needed to centralise its activities. The council wanted its new town hall to be near the centre of Manchester, in a respectable district, close to banks and other municipal offices, and also next to a large open area where public assemblies could be held. To meet these specifications the corporation acquired the 'town yard', a partially built up area, triangular in shape, covered with scruffy grass, next to the neo-gothic Albert Memorial which had been erected in 1862.

To recruit an architect, the city council held a national competition supervised by George Godwin, editor of the prestigious magazine, *The Builder*. Eight semi-finalists were selected, including several of national reputation such as

Cuthbert Broderick (Leeds Corn Exchange), John O. Scott (second son of George Gilbert Scott and noted restorer of churches) and Thomas Henry Wyatt (Knightsbridge Barracks, London). The winner of the final round in 1868 was Alfred Waterhouse (Broad Street façade of Balliol College, Oxford, and later president of the Royal Institute of British Architects).

Controversy followed. Many prominent citizens complained that a more Gothic design, with a greater numer of turrets and pitched roofs, should have been chosen. This judgement seems astonishing today, since it is hard to describe the existing new town hall as anything except Gothic. Nevertheless, the debate underlined Manchester's insistence that its new structure symbolise close connection with the local patriotism of medieval and renaissance city-states.

By spring of 1868, Waterhouse had prepared working drawings for the foundation of his edifice, and contractors began work shortly thereafter. But the entire structure was not to be completed for another ten years, with internal finishings and murals even later. In this respect, the process was like many modern public works projects. It was hampered by arguments, errors and cost overruns. Yet it also resembled the construction of a medieval cathedral. Slowly, persistently it revealed an entire society's concern to give full and proper expression to a guiding vision of life.

An embarrassing episode occurred in 1873. Sensing that they ought to employ a famous artist to decorate the new town hall, Manchester businessmen decided to employ Ford Madox Brown to paint a number of murals for the main assembly room. Artist and city fathers easily agreed that the murals should portray famous episodes in Manchester's history. But they were humiliated when a prominent local antiquarian, W. E. A. Axon, tactfully pointed out that the history the artist was being asked to paint was fiction. Proposals for one mural described a battle in Salford during the English civil war, although the skirmish actually took place at Aldport. Proposals for another mural emphasised the strong support given by Manchester to Prince Charles Edward and the Stuart cause in 1745. Axon claimed that a more accurate version would show the town being rescued for the Loyalist cause by 'a man, a woman, and a boy'. Although Ford Madox Brown's paintings were subsequently completed,

24   Manchester Town Hall, designed by Alfred Waterhouse

the resentment provoked by this episode remained. Shortly before his death in 1893, the town council of Manchester met in private and put forward a resolution to whitewash his murals and replace them with advertisements of locally manufactured products. The resolution was never carried out, but the painter's son, Ford Madox Ford, claims in *Memories and Impressions* (1932 and later, various titles) that news of the resolution caused the apoplectic fit which led to his father's death.

Inclusion of other embelishments proved less difficult. In 1877, as an afterthought not originally proposed by the architect, the city council paid to have a great, hydraulic powered organ installed in the new structure. St Saens was to play on this instrument some years later. No objects in the town hall excited more pride among Manchester citizens than the bells, first installed in 1877. For centuries, bells had been symbols of prestige not only in colleges and churches but in public structures as well. The new town hall contained twenty-one bells, with a combined weight of thirty-four tons, one of the ten largest carillons in the world.

For the grand opening of the new town hall, Manchester greatly desired the attendance of the Queen. Particularly among members of the city's growing Conservative constituency, hope for her presence was almost desperate. Tories had even gone so far as to prevent inclusion of references to Peterloo in Ford Madox Brown's murals, for fear of offending the Queen, even though Liberals and Radicals pointed out that the episode was in many ways a proud part of the city's traditions. But all overtures to the Queen were unsuccessful. The official exchanges can be traced in the Council *Proceedings* from 1867 onwards. Behind the scenes it soon became clear that the Queen had misgivings. Not even Disraeli could persuade her to consent, although he made several attempts, grounded in awareness of his need for the large Conservative vote which Manchester political leaders were now able to deliver at each Parliamentary election. Finally on 31st March 1877, Disraeli relayed the Queen's firm refusal, taking refuge in the cryptic phrases, 'it is out of the power of her Majesty to be present on this interesting occasion'.

The reason commonly given for the Queen's refusal was her general reluctance, ever since the death of Prince Albert, to interrupt mourning by appearing in public ceremonies. But rumours began to spread that the Queen refused because Manchester City Council had voted some years before to erect a statue in memory of Oliver Cromwell. Another explanation was that the Queen was unwilling to be seen on the same platform with Abel Heywood, then mayor of Manchester, who had been involved in radical politics as a young man and had once been imprisoned for circulating publications which advocated overthrow of the monarchy.

Corporate pride was too strong, however, for these setbacks to do much damage. The formal opening of the new town hall, on 13th September 1877, showed Victorian municipal patriotism in elaborate ceremonial detail. Amidst banners hanging everywhere from shops, warehouses, and offices, members of the city council met at 1.30 pm in King Street at the old town hall and began marching three abreast toward Albert Square. All along the route, spectators cheered and waved handkerchiefs. A military band greeted the marchers as they reached the Square and the new municipal bells pealed overhead. Cavalry and infantry flanked the procession. In the best Manchester tradition, inclement weather forced the soldiers to wear dark greatcoats, making the scene less brilliant than it might have been, but even this detail was fitting for a resolute trading city of the north.

At the speaker's platform in front of the new town hall, the town clerk presented a gold key to the mayor and quoted the *Manchester Guardian's* statement of that day that the new town hall 'stands visibly reminding every citizen of Manchester of the labours and responsibilities of the community to which he belongs . . .'

Unlocking the front door, the mayor declared the new town hall open. Bands gave a flourish of trumpets. The infantry presented arms and the cavalry raised their swords. Members of the city council entered the building and walked to their meeting room. The cavalry band played the National Anthem. Then the soldiers retired and the crowd dispersed. Banquets followed throughout the afternoon and evening.

The largest banquet, involving nearly 400 guests, included the Lord Chief Justice of England, seventeen present or former members of Parliament, the mayors of twenty-six other towns and cities, and numerous journalists. James Fraser, the widely respected Anglican Bishop of Manchester, reflected the mood of many Conservatives during his speech at this gathering when he expressed regret that the Queen had not seen fit to recognise by a personal visit that 'one in eight of all the subjects over whom the Queen reigned in these islands' was a resident of Manchester or its immediate environs. He deplored 'those carpings which dainty and witty gentlemen leading a pleasant club life in London indulged in at the expense of Manchester when they told them what a vulgar set of people they were . . .'

But the challenge of capturing the full meaning of the moment was best met, as on so many other occasions, by John Bright. Recalling the shabby disarray of Manchester's local government just fifty years previously, Bright reviewed the progress since that time and praised the 'liberality', 'generosity', and 'municipal freedom' which the New Town Hall symbolised. He hoped that the achievements of local government would be 'spoken of . . . for generations and for centuries' and he urged his listeners to take delight in the 'municipal palace' which they had created. Then, in a note of caution, he advised his audience to remember the economic storms which their city had weathered often in their lifetime. He asked Mancunians to imagine a day when the great new structure before them might lie in ruins, for they 'must bear in mind that great cities have fallen before Manchester and Liverpool were known; that there have been great cities . . . Phoenecia, Carthage, Genoa, Venice. . . And therefore . . . let us not for a moment imagine that we stand upon a foundation absolutely sure and absolutely unmovable . . .'

National reaction to these ceremonies was extensive but subdued. At first there were no comments like those which *The Builder* was to offer much later, in 1896, when it described the new town hall as 'one of the most excellent works which the nineteenth century has bequeathed to its successors'. Judgements at the time of opening were more mixed. For example, in September 1877, *Punch* referred seriously to the opening of 'a magnificent edifice' at Manchester, but mused upon the difficulty of getting the city's leaders to wear clothing sufficiently refined for a formal dress ceremony. *The Times* (14th September 1877) claimed that the new town hall had been constructed 'to provide . . . a suite of civic state apartments such as might relieve the local rulers from too painful a sense of contrast when they thought of the Guildhall or Mansion-House in London'. But the paper granted that Manchester possessed a truly impressive municipal organisation. *The Times* declared, 'All the world has heard of the scale on which Manchester has organised a local administration with many departments – Police, Water Supply, Gas Works, Paving, Sewering, and everything requisite for keeping so great a city in tolerable order . . .'

It was, of course, the positive side of such comments which the populace of Manchester most endorsed. Local pride attained its most fulsome display on the Saturday after the previous evening's banquets and speeches. Some 44,000 working men paraded through the city in the latest of those colourful trades processions which Manchester had conducted over the century. The parade did not include representatives of the very lowest classes of Manchester (in these years before the London dock strike (1889), unskilled labourers were still not unionised to any great extent). The turnout for the parade was nevertheless huge, and indicated, by its remarkable orderliness and enthusiasm, that Manchester enjoyed broad support for the ideals embodied in the new town hall.

The parade began at 11 am and ended four and a half hours later. It was so complex and large that marchers had to divide in three sections and merge gradually with the aid of marshals and constables bearing directional signs. The complete procession stretched for more than three miles. The crowds of onlookers numbered 66,000. One reporter noted, 'Not a window from which a view of the procession could be obtained was without its occupants, and there was no available spot on the tops of the buildings commanding a sight of the display left unutilised' (W. E. A. Axon).

In bright sunshine, a gift of the Nordic weather gods for the previous day's perseverance, the mayor put on his scarlet robe of office and joined the soldiers, their uniforms in full view, at the reviewing stand in Albert Square. In varied, seemingly endless succession, the working class marched by. Filesmiths, boilermakers, lath cleavers, plasterers, meat cutters, power loom overlookers, fine and coarse cotton spinners, beamers, twisters and drawers – these and a hundred other occupations were represented. Many of the workers' organisations marched in time to their own bands. The glass cutters were armed with glass swords while several carried a huge glass cask filled with beer. The printers carried a large banner with the motto 'Let there be light'. The unbrella makers carried a banner with the motto 'Self Protection' as well as a gigantic sample of their work made from the finest gingham. The tailors were dressed stylishly and had flowers in their buttonholes. The bakers carried a loaf of bread weighing 164 pounds. The chimney sweeps, revealing their national background, carried a 'mysterious flag' upon which was an unmistakable likeness of Daniel O'Connell. The carpenters carried a large flag which had first been displayed during the Reform Bill struggle of 1832: on one side it stated in large letters, 'Those who assert that politics will ruin trade unions have yet something to learn'; on the other side it proclaimed, 'Deal with us on the 'square', you have 'chiselled' us long enough'. The coopers carried barrels. The plumbers displayed water fittings. The hammermen and furnacemen carried a large model of a steam hammer, requiring four men to carry it. And, placed indelicately in front of the temperance societies, the coppersmiths carried brass models of a sugar refiner and a whiskey still.

When the parade finally dispersed around 3.30 pm, the marchers made their way to local parks where they received free refreshments and were entertained by local bands and orchestras. Many who had watched the parade joined in. Excursion trains brought more workers from surrounding towns. The temperance societies held their own meeting separately.

That night at 9 pm there was a special display of fireworks, including 'a colossal illumination representing the Albert Square front of the new town hall. The lines of the building were shown in myriads of jets of coloured fires, whilst a separate device contained the arms of the city, with the motto, "Concilio et Labore", and the words, in prominent characters, "Success to the New Town Hall"' (Axon).

When the jubilee of the opening of the new town hall was celebrated in September 1927, the *Manchester Guardian* quoted an anonymous local historian who had penned the following remarks several years after 1877: 'If ever the candlestick be

25   The Trades' Procession to celebrate the opening of Manchester Town Hall on 13th September 1877. Oil Painting

removed from her midst, and the commercial glory of Manchester be extinguished, let us hope that the Town Hall will remain a memento as redolent of high association as those grand old city halls of the Low Countries which still live to speak of a commercial greatness memorable not for itself alone, but from its intimate connection with the loftiest national endeavour.'

CHAPTER 11

National resurrection:
The Manchester Ship Canal

Economic insecurity had been one important force prompting construction of the new town hall. The same insecurity led Manchester to another great contribution to national life in the field of engineering. By the 1870s, Britain was facing increased competition from the factories of Germany and the north-eastern United States. Markets once dominated now had to be shared, not only in the cotton manufacture but in other industries as well. Britain experienced a sharp decline in the balance of trade, even though the nation enjoyed increased prosperity in the 'home trade' and increased purchasing power overseas.

British merchants and manufacturers searched for new markets, tried to purchase raw materials more cheaply from new sources, modernised outmoded factory equipment, lowered the wages of workers, decreased their own profits in many cases, enhanced the quality and attractiveness of their products; offered more favourable terms of credit and diversified into new industries. But none of these approaches restored the nation to the favoured economic status it had enjoyed in the mid-Victorian era.

Businessmen were, therefore, extremely interested when Manchester presented them with a daring and original method of economic renewal – a strategy not available to all localities, yet which provided hints and inspiration for all who sought to find their way out of economic perplexity.

For many decades, Manchester businessmen had been trying to lower the costs of transporting goods between their city and Liverpool, which was in effect Manchester's harbour and its major point of contact with the world. If dock charges in Liverpool and railway rates between the two cities could be decreased, then Manchester would become more competitive in international markets and be able, as well, to offer lower prices to British customers. But the dock interests in Liverpool and the railway in London were not sympathetic to such proposals and continued business as usual, secure in the knowledge that Manchester needed them and was forced to pay their prices.

Manchester businessmen decided, therefore, to connect their city via a huge ship canal with the open sea. They realised that such a scheme would not supplant the need for use of railways in the home trade – from Manchester to London, for example – and they knew it would not provide the advantages of simply moving Manchester's factories to Liverpool – perhaps the best long-term solution, but initially very expensive, and risky because of the special climate required for spinning and weaving cotton. Nevertheless, the potential economic benefits of such a canal were enormous.

The idea had, in fact, been a subject of discussion in Manchester for many years. Ready at hand was the example of the Bridgewater Canal, completed in 1722 to lower the cost of transporting coal from the Duke of Bridgewater's properties west of Manchester to purchasers in the growing town. The Duke's canal had caused great excitement in its early days and continued to be profitable. Other schemes appeared later. In 1825, for example, a William Chapman approached Parliament for authoruty to build a Manchester Ship canal, and another serious proposal, from one Henry Palmer, received attention in 1840.

By 1869, when the Suez canal opened, large canals were of interest not only to Manchester but to most of the world. In 1887, the German government began construction of the Kiel canal, opened in 1895. In America and in France, flamboyant entrepreneurs were already taking the steps that would result in the Panama canal, opened in 1914 after a decade of construction.

To transform its own scheme for a ship canal from dream to reality, Manchester needed leadership of the kind that had propelled the Anti-Corn Law League and other great initiatives. In 1882, Daniel Adamson, a prominent Manchester citizen and engineer of world reputation, decided to offer his talents. He convened a meeting in the baronial setting of the wood-panelled library at 'The Towers,' his neo-Gothic mansion in one of Manchester's wealthy suburbs. Some seventy prominent persons attended, representing Manchester and thirteen factory towns in Lancashire. Speaking in what one eye-witness called 'a strong Northumbrian burr', and what another contemporary called 'the Doric accent of the North', Adamson outlined the advantages which had followed improvement of other rivers – the Tyne, the Tees, and the Clyde – and said that improving the Mersey and the Irwell would be an easy task compared to construction of the Suez canal.

A few of Adamson's listeners reacted sceptically, most notably C. P. Scott, the influential editor of the *Manchester Guardian*. But most of the guests responded like the mayor of Salford, who said he 'did not believe that there would be a grander sight under the canopy of Heaven than the docks at Manchester crowded with shipping from all parts of the world'. Immediately after the meeting Adamson began a speaking tour of northern business centres to attract investors.

The press quickly saw the colour and drama of the proposal. One Liverpool newspaper declared that the object of the canal promoters was 'the complete annihilation of Liverpool'. *Punch* published a full-page cartoon of the proposed canal (7th October 1882), with the caption 'Manchester-sur-Mer: A Sea-ductive Prospect', showing a voluptuous maiden at the seashore, well-covered in a Victorian bathing suit, with the waters of the canal lapping at her feet. *The Times* (18th October) declared, five millions and a half of people are at the mercy of a combination holding a pass between them and the rest of the human race, and making use of the coin of vantage as the medieval barons did in the embattled toll-gates thrown across the world's highways'. A large cartoon appeared in *Tit Bits* showing 'The Port of Manchester in 1950', intersected by numerous waterways, and covered by a sprawl of notably unfuturistic factories . The *Illustrated London News* (3rd February 1883) included a full-colour fold-out map showing the course of the proposed canal.

Comment took on a deeper meaning as observers began to see in Manchester's scheme a key to solving the nation's larger

26   Daniel Adamson, a painting in Manchester Town Hall

economic problems. When *The Saturday Review* endorsed the canal proposal (4th November 1882), it sensed the large forces involved, noting that in 1880, 'not far short of one-third of the whole foreign trade of the United Kingdom passed through Liverpool'. *The Contemporary Review* declared (April 1883), 'It will be well if out of this provincial ebullition we may gain a hint as to national policy'. For the *Review,* the canal scheme provided inspiring reminders of the skill in competition which Britain had once shown through free trade and *laissez-faire.* No more than Britain endorsed artificially high pricing policies by other nations should it tolerate such behaviour by its own dock and railway owners. The *Review* intoned, 'That which is moving South Lancashire as an aggrieved district, should move us all as a trading nation'.

It was only a short step from such homilies to the claim of Sir William Fairbairn, the internationally famous engineer, in a widely circulated pamphlet of 1883, that enabling ocean vessels to dock at Manchester would 'quadruple her population, and render her the first, as well as the most enterprising, city of Europe'.

All this, of course, was speculation, for in 1883 the provisional committee formed by Daniel Adamson still faced basic tasks. Most important was selection of a method for constructing the canal. Two strategies had been considered. Hamilton and Fulton, a civil engineering firm based in London, proposed to bring the ocean directly to Manchester via a tide canal which would be formed by straightening, widening and deepening the Mersey and Irwell rivers. This plan offered speed and relatively low cost. But since Manchester is sixty feet above sea level, ships at the Manchester end of such a canal would have had to dock in a deep crater, hoisting and lowering their cargoes with great difficulty and at great expense. For these reasons, the provisional committee instead adopted the strategy of lifting ships from the Mersey to Manchester in a series of locks which would roughly parallel the Irwell and in a few places enter or cross it. Planning for a canal of this kind was entrusted to Leader Williams, a Manchester engineer with previous experience in canal construction.

To go forward with any plan, the provisional committee was required by law to obtain approval from Parliament. This it undertook in 1883. Negotiations were to last two years. One contemporary journalist called the manoeuvrings surrounding the Ship Canal Bill 'the most arduous and protracted fight in the annals of private bill legislation'. It was estimated that the battle cost the proponents of the Bill £150,000, while the opponents spent an additional £200,000-£250,000. In one parliamentary session, 25,367 questions concerning the Bill were asked in the Lords' committee, with answers filling 1,861 pages. By 1885, when the struggle finally ended, it had consumed 175 days of parliamentary business. Perhaps the nearest twentieth-century equivalent to this battle would be one of the lobbying efforts involving arms manufacture or an aircraft project such as the Concorde, in which professional careers and the future of entire economic regions seem to participants to be at stake.

The chief opponents of the Ship Canal Bill were the railway companies and the Corporation and Dock Board of Liverpool. While these interests were in the long run unsuccessful, they did succeed in persuading Parliament to require expensive changes in the route of the canal, a precaution against possible alterations in the current of the Mersey and silting which would have clogged Liverpool's harbour.

As finally passed by Parliament in 1885, the Ship Canal Bill called for a channel thirty-five-and-a-half feet long, at least twenty-six feet deep at all points, 120 feet wide at the bottom, and an average width of 172 feet at water level – which would widen as the canal neared Manchester to 170 feet at the bottom and 230 feet at water level. This compared with a depth of twenty-six feet for the Suez Canal, although the Suez channel was not more than seventy-two feet wide at any point.

Throughout the parliamentary hearings, municipal and regional patriotism was intense. It even led to public boycotts of merchants opposed to the Bill. In October 1885, to celebrate passage of the Bill, Manchester held a great trades procession similar to that which had opened the new town hall. The American journalist H. M. Stanley happened to be in Manchester at the time. He asked why the procession was occurring and was told simply, 'Manchester has gone mad'.

Included in the Ship Canal Bill as finally passed was the requirement that all necessary capital be raised by 1887, not only to finance construction but to purchase the Bridgewater canal as well. This amounted to £5,000,000 in share capital for the first purpose and a further £1,700,000 for the second. At first the promoters hoped to obtain a loan in the London market through assistance from the Rothschild interests. This scheme failed. Rumours circulated that the Rothschild interests had capitulated to pressures from Liverpool dock owners and the railway companies. A modern authority, David Owen, argues that London bankers had rightly noted technical flaws in the way the bonds had been drawn up.

The promoters next tried the strategy of appointing a committee of prominent citizens to review pros and cons of constructing the canal. This committee's report was favourable, but scepticism remained, and so the Canal promoters took the additional step of issuing preference shares of stock. With this key move, the Rothschild interests endorsed the project and, just days before the deadline of 6th August 1887, adequate funding was raised.

Construction began shortly thereafter, supervised by Thomas Walker, the engineer who had constructed the Severn tunnel and several sections of the London Underground railway system.

Groundbreaking took place in late 1887 at Eastham, a quiet rural village in rolling green countryside at the end of the canal nearest Liverpool. The 'cutting of the first sod', as a local journalist termed it, took place on 'a cheerless November day . . . in a way characteristic of Manchester men in earnest. There was no ceremonial, no spectators, and no speeches. Even the spade which was used was an ordinary spade which had seen some service and was to see more.'

But as construction proceeded more visitors appeared. London journalists toured the area, as did American engineers and royal figures from abroad. Also among prominent sightseers was William Gladstone. In 1889, between terms as Prime Minister, he viewed the works and then addressed a luncheon in Manchester given by the mayor. As Liverpool's most important son, he declared tactfully that the canal would cause his city 'no damage whatever' and would give all British cities an example of 'heroism' inspiring 'the nation at large' to great achievements.

27 Manchester Ship Canal under construction
28 'Manchester-sur-mer. A sea-ductive prospect'.
    Cartoon from *Punch* 7th October 1882

In November, 1889, the canal contractor, Thomas Walker, died. He had left instructions in his will for completing his work. Nevertheless, by the summer of 1890, angry disagreements had developed between Walker's executors and the canal company, and by November the directors had decided to assume supervision of the work. Even though Walker's staff remained on the job and in the employ of the canal company, efficiency was lessened. By January 1891, in addition, the directors had begun to see that either they or Walker had made a serious error by purchasing more land for the canal than was necessary. At the same time, costs were rising because of delays in construction caused by heavy rains and unexpected changes from the original plan. Thus, the total of £10 million capital authorised to complete the project would not be enough.

The directors decided that there was no chance of raising all the new capital necessary on the open market. They turned to the City of Manchester. After extensive public hearings, the Manchester Corporation agreed to advance the canal company up to £3 million if necessary.

In some ways, this was a stern bargain. The city council insisted on being the first creditor in line, superseding the holders of the £8 million share capital previously authorised. The Manchester Corporation insisted, as well, that the canal company cease payment of interest to shareholders out of capital; which by that time amounted to £490,000. The city government also retained the right to appoint five representatives to the canal company's board of directors. In return, the corporation agreed to borrow money for the canal company at 3½ per cent, with the canal company repaying it to the city at 4½ per cent.

Nevertheless, after analysing the statistical projections upon which the Manchester Corporation's actions had been based, a contemporary writer for the *Yale Review* (November 1894) commented, 'Never in the history of a great engineering undertaking in England were the estimates more deplorably at fault'. In the writer's opinion, Manchester had been swayed by 'civic pride.' Had the city 'desired to make the best possible bargain from a commercial point of view, it would have allowed the canal company to have gone into bankruptcy'.

By 1892 construction of the Ship Canal was almost three-quarters done. Observers could now appreciate the enormity of the work. A reporter for *Good Words* (February 1892) described to his audience of middle-class families the elemental quality of the project. In epic terms, he saw Thomas Walker, who had directed construction in early years, as 'a prince among contractors', involved in 'Herculean labours', directing 'regiments' of 'as many as seventeen thousand men and boys . . . at one time'. These burly labourers 'made one proud to think that such magnificent limbs are still made in England'. Also at the contractor's command, the reporter noted, were some 100 steam navvies – mechanical shovels – plus 173 railway locomotives and 6,330 waggons. The writer claimed, 'such a large and various collection of implements for an assault upon mother earth has never been brought together before'.

Exhiliration over the economic example provided by the Ship Canal also reached new heights. The *St James's Gazette* declared (1893), 'Manchester declines to decline. It is such things as the Manchester Ship Canal and the [Firth of] Forth Bridge which ought somewhat to cheer the pessimist who looks round and tells us of the decadence of Great Britain.' *Chamber's Journal* (December 1893) said that the Ship Canal surpassed all the 'bold and successful industrial innovations' for which Manchester had been responsible in the past. The canal would 'form an epoch in the history of British trade and manufactures', making the Suez canal seem 'a mere ditch.'

The official business opening of the canal came on New Year's Day 1894, accompanied by speeches, private dinners and a small ceremony. But the true confirmation of the project's symbolic importance came in May 1894, when the Queen arrived in Manchester for special ceremonies. She had not visited Manchester since the time of the Art Treasures Exhibition, almost forty years before.

On the morning of Monday, 21st May 1894, the Queen left Windsor for Manchester by train, accompanied by members of the royal family and several railway company executives attempting to make the best of new realities. Six hours later the Queen arrived at London Road station, Manchester, where she was met by a reception committee and a guard of honour of mounted police and artillery volunteers. Proceeding in her carriage to the new town hall, she told a large crowd of her hope 'that all classes and subjects may share in the benefits attending on the success of this most important enterprise'. Riding several blocks to the Municipal Schools of Art, she gave similarly bland words of congratulations and, in the best Manchester tradition, found herself in a sudden cloudburst.

Around 6 pm the Queen's party arrived at the Ship Canal docks at Trafford Road where the Queen's yacht *Enchantress* was waiting. She knighted the lord mayor of Manchester and the mayor of Salford and then pushed a button that was connected electrically to the Canal locks, saying, 'I have now great pleasure in declaring the Manchester Ship Canal open'. A salute of twenty-one guns followed, and then a brief tour aboard *Enchantress* of the canal's waters. This ceremony completed, the Queen rode in her carriage from Trafford Wharf to Salford where she received a loyal address from the mayor. Finally she made her way to Exchange station in Manchester, departing the city at 7.30 pm.

As these details indicate, the Queen's entire visit was perfunctory. Clearly she still felt no warmth for Manchester, but the fact that she had come at all was perhaps the most telling evidence of the Ship Canal's importance for the nation. Gratified if not elated, the city fathers of Manchester retired after her departure to a large banquet at which the lord mayor of Liverpool praised them for the estimable British virtue of 'dogged persistency'.

National attention subsided gradually thereafter. There were occasional notes on the canal's operations in the periodical press, perhaps the most interesting being an article of 1896 in *Pearson's Magazine,* which portrayed Manchester, now a duly constituted seaport, as one of the 'Gates and Pillars of the Empire'. But in fact the only question that still aroused public curiosity was whether the canal would be a financial success.

At first it was not. Ship traffic gradually increased, but not rapidly enough to prevent the canal company from operating at a loss. The first great economic benefit of the canal was, in fact, not even one that had been intended. By greatly facilitating haulage of heavy freight, the canal made it possible for Manchester to become a great centre of engineering. The canal also greatly stimulated the development of food warehousing in and about the city, as it became more efficient to load and unload imported agricultural products in Manchester rather

29 Queen Victoria at the opening of the Manchester Ship Canal
21st May 1894

30 Manchester Docks

than Liverpool, previously the major distribution centre for feeding the vast industrial population of Lancashire. As had been predicted, railway rates did go down, and the dock interests of Liverpool did lower their rates and improve their services. But this was not enough. Even when priced more competitively, the cotton goods of Manchester and its region continued to win only a declining share of the world market. The canal itself did not pay until over two decades after it opened, when the First World War cataclysmically altered the international system of economic relationships.

CHAPTER 12

The Manchester man

In praising the Ship Canal, Englishmen were voicing respect, above all, for the qualities of determination and daring which individual Manchester residents such as Daniel Adamson had displayed during its construction. By the end of the nineteenth century, the same focus upon particular traits of Manchester character was visible in many other areas of national life. To some degree, all cities stamp their inhabitants with distinct personalities which set the residents of one city off from another. But Manchester in the nineteenth century was an unuaually clear example of this process, and no history of the Victorian city would be complete without attention to the phenomenon.

The lingering stereotype. One of the earliest recorded attacks upon the personality produced by the Manchester environment appeared in *Blackwood's Edinburgh Magazine* in April and May issues, 1821. Of one of its Manchester correspondents, *Blackwood's* said: 'Being a native of Manchester, he is of course completely familiarized to the climate, and having the intellectual constitution of a horse, he can bear the conversation even of Manchester cotton spinners without flinching.' *Blackwood's* added: 'There is something in the very name [of Manchester] itself which puts to flight all poetical associations . . . The only association we have connected with this very commercial town is the abstract idea of a little whey-faced man, in a brown frock-coat and dirty coloured neckcloth, smelling . . . of cottons and callicoes [sic]; talking, not of poetry or the stagyrite, but of nine-tenths and fustians; and writing – not of Shakespeare or Pope, but "Your's of the 11th ult. duly came to hand, in which per advice, &c, &c"'.

Similar attacks recurred throughout the nineteenth century, in spite of protests from Manchester residents that they distorted the truth. By the 1870s, however, they no longer reflected the dominant opinion of the public, as was shown in a celebrated controversy concerning enlargement of Manchester's water supply. The corporation of the City of Manchester had begun plans for construction of a long line of pipes and acqueducts between the city proper and Thirlmere in the Lake District, ninety-six miles to the north. Manchester already had access to some water from the Pennines, due to an earlier engineering project, completed in the 1850s, involving the Longdendale valley. To meet growing demand, however, the city was seeking additional sources.

The Thirlmere scheme enjoyed wide public approval. But news of its adoption aroused the anger of a number of prominent British intellectuals, including J. R. Seeley, the historian, and John Ruskin. All shared a reverence for the unspoiled beauty of the Lake District and a temperamental dislike of the uglier features of industrial society. Led by Ruskin, they banded together in a small but energetic movement opposing implementation of the Thirlmere project. The strategy for gaining supporters was use of the decades-old vision of Manchester as a place of great rawness. A passage from one of Ruskin's famous essays, in *Fors Clavigera,* published in 1877, shows the technique in sophisticated form: 'Taken as a whole, I perceive that Manchester can produce no good art, and no good literature; it is falling off even in the quality of its cotton; it has reversed and vilified in loud lies, every essential principle of Political Economy; it is cowardly in war, predatory in peace; and as a corporate body, plotting at last to steal, and sell, for a profit, the waters of Thirlemere and clouds of Helvellyn.' By such rhetorical blasts, critics of the Thirlmere project did manage to cause a few problems for Manchester's reputation. In fact, however, sufficient opposition could not be mobilised, and the Thirlmere scheme proceeded from plan to actual construction.

The flaw in Ruskin's strategy was its timing. Twenty years earlier, readers agreeing with his anti-Manchester prose probably would have been available in great numbers. By the 1870s, however, Ruskin's views regarding Manchester were shared chiefly by those who joined him in making aesthetics, conservation of the natural environment and a return to pre-industrial forms of community the primary values in life. Thus, Manchester became a frequent stop on speaking tours for the utopian socialist, William Morris, and Robert Blatchford, who propounded similar ideas in more popular, journalistic form, devoted great attention to Manchester in his writings. In the third chapter of *Merrie England* (1894), which sold over two million copies and became an inspiration for socialists in the United States and Europe, Blatchford railed against 'the Manchester school' and hypocritical Manchester factory owners who forced their workers to live in slums lacking 'pure air, bright skies, clear rivers, clean streets, and beautiful fields', but who themselves retreated to suburbs 'as far from the factories as they can get'. Still later, in 1910, in a pamphlet circulated both in Britain and the United States, Blatchford seized upon Chetham College, the medieval Gothic structure preserved in central Manchester, as 'the sole remnant of grace and dignity left in this great vulgar city, in this blatant pursy age'. Somewhat fancifully, he characterised the College's library as the 'haunt of the little band of poets and thinkers who survive in Modern Athens like the few grayling lingering in a stream befouled'.

The Manchester man: early and late Victorian. Although influential, the writings of Ruskin and Blatchford showed no awareness of the complex transitions through which public perceptions of Manchester's residents had gone since the early nineteenth century. The habit of ascribing distinct traits to Manchester residents in fact preceded the industrialisation of the city. Originally, 'Manchester men' had been the travelling peddlers who carried their wares by packhorse to Cheshire and Derbyshire and across the hazardous, robber-infested Pennines to the north-eastern counties of England. As the cotton industry expanded, more sophisticated methods of warehousing and marketing resulted in the disappearance of these itinerant salesmen. The term 'Manchester man' continued to be part of popular speech, but took on a different meaning that was clear by the 1820s. In the narrowest sense, the new usage referred specifically to a successful cotton manufacturer or merchant who had won the respect of fellow townspeople, the most accepted sign of such respect being membership in the Manchester Exchange, where most of the city's business was transacted. In its broader meaning, the term referred to a combination of elements which were assumed to form Manchester's personality. Cobden and Bright, often thought of as 'Manchester men' by the broad public, illustrated the type: earnest, hardworking, self-righteous, a bit dull in matters of art and whimsy, morally concerned and puritanical in religion even if occasionally not a member of any dissenting sect.

These traits were 'codified', one might say, in 1874, when *Cassell's Family Magazine* published in instalments 'The Manchester man,' by Mrs G. Linnaeus Banks (Isabella Varley Banks), the wife of a Manchester businessman and a writer of local note. Set in Manchester in the years 1790-1830, the novel tells the story of an abandoned baby found floating on the waters of the River Irwell, who is given the name Jabez Clegg, and who grows to manhood in the home of a humble working-class family, overcomes personal tragedies, and becomes a prosperous cotton merchant able to take his place as a 'Manchester man' in the upper circles of the growing city's cultural, social and economic life. Neither the characters of the novel nor its plot are impressive. Filled with stock villains, deathbed scenes, and wooden dialogue, the work is stereotypical Victorian melodrama.

Nevertheless, *The Manchester Man* is distinguished by the author's detailed descriptions of the city of the early industrial era. One does come away from the story with a clearer picture of Peterloo, the rise of the cotton industry, the sudden appearance of new streets and buildings, the living conditions of workers, and other aspects of the history which form the story's background. For these reasons *The Manchester Man* was sufficiently well received to be published in book form and to enjoy profitable if not awesome sales for many years thereafter. Even today, the novel is still reprinted, and it has taken its place as a 'regional classic,' an example of that genre in which England is so abundant.

Although it chronicled the rough-hewn, early era of industrial Manchester, *The Manchester Man* was in fact proof of growing refinement in Manchester people. It reminded readers that industrial Manchester had history. And, by self-consciously focusing upon a 'Manchester man' of an earlier generation, it implied that there were important differences between Manchester people of the past and those of the 1870s. If Jabez Clegg and his world could be seen as quaint and charming, then the implication had to be that present-day Manchester men had transcended his shortcomings. If Jabez Clegg could be admired for his energy and initiative, then the implication was that present-day Manchester residents could still empathise with his drive, but could blend it with the virtues of more civilised urban dwellers. By the time Mrs Banks' novel appeared, Englishmen had already begun to recognise that refinement might be one quality of a Manchester man.

The Manchester Irishman. For most of the nineteenth century, the term 'Manchester man' tacitly omitted the Irish. They formed perhaps one-third of the city's population by the late Victorian era and were a major source of cheap labour. Catholics, mostly of peasant background, and heirs to several centuries of hatred between themselves and English rulers, they did not mix well in Manchester Nonconformist circles and formed their own alienated community. Under the law they enjoyed at least a measure of religious toleration, but by the 1850s they had made Manchester into an enclave of Irish political separatism second only to London in importance. The most dramatic outbreak of this antagonism in Manchester took place in September 1867, when a group of thirty Fenians, members of the militant Irish Republican Brotherhood which had secret chapters throughout Britain and the United States, attacked a prison van that was carrying two IRB leaders implicated in rebellions of the preceding March. The two prisoners broke free, but only after a Manchester police sergeant had been shot dead, some thought accidentally. Three of the instigators of the ambush, Michael Larkin, William Allen and Michael O'Brien, were captured and sentenced to death in spite of a lack of evidence that their weapons had caused the policeman's death.

The three were hanged in Manchester in November 1867. Many Englishmen considered this a strategic blunder by the government, since death sentences in similar instances had been commuted after risings in other localities in 1848 and 1867.

The three Fenians quickly became known as the 'Manchester martyrs'. Angry mass meetings were held throughout Ireland and in Irish communities in Britain and the United States. A song entitled 'God save Ireland' was composed in honour of the 'martyrs' and was sung for the next fifty years almost as if it were a national anthem, while in Manchester the events of 1867 aroused memories for many years that were as strong as those of Peterloo.

The relations of individual Irish and English in Victorian Manchester were varied and complex, showing virtually every permutation from hatred to love, from complete misunderstanding to mutual respect. No single document captures the full story. One particularly illuminating example of possibilities, however, is *My Son, My Son,* the best-selling novel by Howard Spring. The book sold well throughout the world, was translated into many languages, and has been reissued many times. It is probably the most competent and moving of Spring's many works and contains the best of his many portrayals of North Country characters.

Although *My Son, My Son* was published in 1938, the narration bridges the late nineteenth and early twentieth centuries, beginning in the 1870s and trailing off in the 1920s. The story tells of the painful relationship between two Manchester residents, Bill Essex and Dermot O'Riorden, and their sons Oliver Essex and Rory O'Riorden. Bill Essex is an almost classic example of Manchester temperament. He is dour, slow-speaking, stoical, hard-working, long-suffering, respectful of education, interested in advancing his social rank, and a great lover of music. As a homeless boy he is given lodgings by a kindly Irish clerk. He becomes the friend of the clerk's son, Dermot O'Riorden, and the lives of the two are intertwined thereafter.

Dermot is witty, quick-tempered, shy but often lyrical, and fully at home in the fine arts, which he uses to make a living in furniture making and handicrafts. Bill Essex and Dermot O'Riorden improve their lot together. Essex learns how to relax and to understand his own emotions through O'Riorden, who encourages his English friend to become a novelist writing about Manchester. O'Riorden in turn benefits handsomely from Essex's loyalty and innate sense of business. At his workshop

in Manchester O'Riorden shows Essex several fascinating chil-
drens' toys he has designed almost as an afterthought. Essex
immediately realises the possibilities and calls upon Manchester's resources to put together the financial and manufacturing
support needed to catapult himself and O'Riorden into a lucra-
tive business partnership. Eventually the two move to London
and reap even larger rewards, Essex as a playwright and O'Riorden as a prominent designer and devotee of William Morris.

A continuing element of strain between the two friends is the
issue of Irish political independence. O'Riorden is inflamed by
memories of the Manchester Martyrs and continuing news of
violence between Irish and British. He is also in close contact
with Irish revolutionaries. He and Essex argue about Ireland
often. But they work very hard to keep the subject from
destroying their friendship. When the First World War breaks
out and the possibility arises of Ireland siding with Germany,
O'Riorden tells Essex: 'Bill, you've often heard me say: "God
damn England," Well, now I say: "God help England," and that's
a prayer . . . This is not a bad country . . . And, begod . . . we
could have it out with you afterwards.'

This fragile unity is not assisted by the two ill-fated sons.
Oliver fails in business, steals away his father's fiancée, and,
after the Great War, drifts into work in Ireland, where he is a
member of the hated British security forces, the Black and Tans.
Here he runs across Rory O'Riorden, who has become a violent
Irish revolutionary acting out the anger his father merely
voiced. Through a series of tragic coincidences, Oliver shoots
and kills Rory in a raid upon a village hideout. Then, a few
years later, Oliver turns up in Manchester where, desperate for
money, he commits robbery and murder and is hanged.

The novel ends as Bill Essex contemplates visiting the graves
of both Oliver and Rory. 'Perhaps Dermot will come with me',
Bill Essex muses. The statement can be seen not only as an
expression of Essex's difficulty in understanding life, but as a
symbol of the irresolution which still prevails in relations
between the Irish and the English.

Other minorities.   If the Irish were perceived as Manchester
men only gradually, then certain other important groups
occupied an even more ambiguous position. One important fact,

known by all but seldom embodied in the term 'Manchester man', was the large foreign element in the city's population. German cultural societies prospered thanks to several generations of Hanseatic migrants who had marketed their skills successfully in Manchester and risen to power in the life of the city. Italians and French had been given refuge in Manchester and other British cities after the revolutions of 1848. Greeks, Arabs, Jews and Egyptians brought knowledge of the cotton trade in the Middle East. A small group of Indians and other Asians appeared as ties with the empire increased.

For the most part, the result was friendly, productive interaction. English residents of Manchester enjoyed the fact that Italians decorated their city with mosaics and frescoes, and they respected the right of Jews and others to build their own places of worship and to practice religion as they saw fit. In spite of the occasional community quarrels, alienation never reached the bitterness shown between English and Irish residents. And yet, the curious fact remained. No one thought of Greeks or Italians or other minorities when speaking of 'Manchester men'.

The Manchester woman.   Equally ironic was the willingness of Victorians to use a specifically male label such as 'Manchester man' as their capsule description for a population which obviously included both sexes. This situation gradually changed, however, due to the leadership of one particularly dynamic Manchester woman.

Emmeline Goulden, the oldest of five daughters of a prosperous Manchester cotton manufacturer, was born in Manchester in 1858. By that time, as an outgrowth of its long tradition of liberal politics, the city already possessed a vigorous minority of crusaders for women's rights. One of their more notable successes was the opening of Owens College to women and another was the creation of the Manchester High School for Girls. In her autobiography, *My Own Story* (1914), the future political activist confirmed the influences of this aspect of Manchester life when she expalined that 'my development into an advocate of militancy was largely a sympathetic process . . .' Blessed with 'love and a comfortable home' during childhood, she began nevertheless 'instinctively to feel that there was

31   Mrs Pankhurst

something lacking', and she recalled being deeply affected by such events as 'a great bazaar which was held in my native city of Manchester . . . to raise money to relieve the poverty of the newly emancipated negro slaves in the United States'.

Emmeline went to finishing school in Paris where her closest friend was the daughter of the Marquis de Rochefort, noted duellist and one of the leaders of the Paris Commune of 1871. The Marquis and his daughter inspired her with a love of liberty. Her education confronted her with the French practice of regarding women as cultural if not legal equals.

Returning to Manchester, she became active in suffrage groups then forming in the city. Through these contacts she met Richard Marsden Pankhurst, a prominent Manchester barrister and author of the first parliamentary bill proposing the vote for women, the Women's Disabilities Removal Bill, introduced in 1879 in the House of Commons by Jacob Bright, MP for Manchester (the brother of John Bright). In 1879 Emmeline Goulden and Richard Pankhurst were married.

In 1886, at Emmeline's insistence, the family moved to London to be closer to the political and legal machinery which might aid the suffrage movement. In the same year the two assisted Mrs Annie Besant in the strike of women workers in London match factories.

Most of Mr Pankhurst's legal business continued to be in Manchester, and to ease the strain of railway commuting he and his wife returned there in 1893, by now with five children. In 1894 Mrs Pankhurst was elected to membership of the local Board of Poor Law Guardians, and she was shocked by the male majority's attention to such aspects of workhouse management as nutrition, treatment of young mothers and care of old people. The experience reinforced her conviction that women would need to represent themselves at the polls and in the professions before such conditions could be charged.

When Mrs Pankhurst's husband died in 1898, she took a salaried appointment, arranged by friends, as registrar of births and deaths in Manchester. This work brought her into contact with all sectors of the population and provided more evidence of inequality. In 1900 she ran successfully for the Manchester School Board, where she spoke out against the practice of paying lower wages to women teachers and publicised the fact that

Manchester Technical College, considered one of the best in Europe, offered almost no technical training for women, even in such activities as the baking and confectionary trades, due to pressures from male-dominated labour unions.

In 1903, Christabel, Mrs Pankhurst's eldest child, completed studies and received her Law degree from Manchester University, even though women were not then allowed to practice law. In that same year, at Mrs Pankhurst's home in Nelson Street in Manchester, the Women's Social and Political Union (WSPU) was founded. Its physical headquarters remained in Manchester until 1906 when the focus of activities shifted to London and Parliament. The rest of Mrs Pankhurst's story, and that of her daughters, belongs not to Victorian Manchester but to the twentieth century and the world.

Workers, the continuing omission. Rights of women, religious toleration, the Irish, Mrs G. Linnaeus Banks, the views of utopian socialists – all these topics of Victorian conversation were important for an understanding of Manchester's collective personality but overlooked one other subject, the self-perceptions of average English workers, which ought to have been included if portraits of Manchester men were to be complete. It is a revealing fact of Victorian life that few workers attempted to or were even asked to describe themselves at length. There were occasional exceptions, such as Samuel Bamford's *Passages in the Life of a Radical* (1844). For the most part, however, the Manchester man was whoever and whatever the middle and upper classes said he was. He was dissected in numerous parliamentary surveys, recorded in paintings and photographs, and dramatically present during strikes, library openings and trade processions. Only in the twentieth century, however, has he begun to find his own complex voice in recollections such as Robert Roberts' two descriptions of Edwardian and Georgian working-class life in Manchester, *The Classic Slum* (1971) and *A Ragged Schooling* (1976).

The social and economic framework of workers' lives in now being charted in studies by twentieth-century historians who have partially reconstructed that world through patient, dedicated assembly of fragmentary details. Some of the better works of this kind are listed in the bibliography (below, pp.

200-206). But perhaps more useful in showing the personalities of workers in late Victorian Manchester are surviving eyewitness accounts by unusually sensitive observers from other classes, most of them forgotten today, who help us to compensate for the absence of a late Victorian J. P. Kay, an Elizabeth Gaskell or an Engels. These accounts show the perplexity and pain of life in Victorian Manchester, but also, in spite of economic deprivation, an ability to survive and find joy thanks to strengths of character similar to those exhibited in more refined form amongst members of the city's middle class.

That life for Manchester workers involved suffering and even terror was amply documented. A typical late nineteenth-century discussion of this fact was included in a series about Manchester in 1900 in *Sunday at Home* magazine, published by the Religious Tract Society of London. The journal found 'public spirit' and 'enterprise' visible in all classes in Manchester, declaring that, in this sense, Manchester people exhibited 'the national characteristics which have created modern England'. It also lauded the remarkable desire for education present in all classes, commenting, 'in addition to Ruskin, Goethe, and positivist societies we have, to cite a few of those less frequently found, Conchological, Cryptogramic, Philatelic and other organisations . . .'. And it noted the support for charitable lodging houses and newly constructed workers' dwellings by a concerned minority of middle and upper-class citizens, taking these as proof of 'the distance that has been traversed in the last half century', and reminding readers that 'the search-light of modern investigation makes the blots on our civilisation more palpable'. But *Sunday at Home* also noted the many slum districts in Manchester, 'simply flooded with beer houses', where public drunkenness was a problem 'far worse' than that in most other large British cities. The article commented upon the 'lack of open spaces', the 'monotonous and treeless' streets, and the many houses 'of a revolting character' which formed the workers' daily environment. It also documented the neglect of working-class children, telling the story, for example, of one boy who was 'rescued' by one of the charity societies and who 'had not the slightest idea how to kiss when he was brought in; his mother had tried to strangle him, and afterwards had tried to drown him in the canal; hence the

32   Children waiting for a procession in Angel Meadow, one of the worst slums in Manchester, in the 1890's

little chap had for some time quite a horror of a bath'.

Other aspects of Manchester's dark underside were vividly portrayed by the Irish-Italian, Jerome Caminada, chief detective inspector of the Manchester police, in his memoir *Twenty-five Years of Detective Life* (1895). Caminada's Manchester was a world of burglars, prostitutes, confidence men, quacks, pickpockets, counterfeiters, beggars organised to exploit the generous, occasional spies at local armaments factories, and gin shops on numerous shabby streets in slums which stretched for miles. 'Few cities in the world have within them so many thieves as Manchester', Caminada wrote. 'The pavement of Cottonopolis is incessantly trodden by rogues', he added. Caminada's reminiscences are at times melodramatic. Moreover, the level and frequency of violence in Victorian Manchester was probably not as high as in cities of the late twentieth century. Caminada himself carried a gun only occasionally. Nevertheless, his memoirs, like the articles in *Sunday at Home,* demonstrate that Manchester was afflicted with severe social problems which dictated that workers develop the personal traits of cleverness, quick perception of danger and willingness to use physical force.

Given such tensions, it is not suprising that desire for escape was an important element in the character of many Manchester workers. The novelist George Gissing (1857-1903) captured this aspect of Manchester life in *Born in Exile* (1892), a heavily autobiographical work based on Gissing's years in the city, first at a Quaker academy in Alderley Edge, then at Owens College, from which Gissing was expelled after being charged with petty thievery to support his mistress. *Born in Exile* is the story of a poor working-class student, Godwin Peak, who attends 'Whitelaw College' in the city of 'Kingsmill' thanks to generous financial support from the college's founder. The novel traces Peak's efforts to transcend his lower-class background, first in Kingsmill/Manchester, then in London and on the Continent, where, after an unhappy marriage and career as a clergyman, Peak dies alone in a hotel room in Vienna. The story focuses on the theme of alienation from stultifying bourgeois values, a favourite concern of intellectuals in the 1890s and since. But Peak is just as afraid of being trapped in the life of working-class Manchester as he is of middle-class rigidity. In the novel's early scenes he castigates the rich of Manchester for failing to provide more scholarships for working-class children. Contact with his uncle, who retains a lower-class accent and mannerisms, makes Peak repeatedly uneasy. And Peak expresses the fear that he will fall into 'the abyss' of the urban underworld just as one of his more distant relatives did early in Peak's life.

And yet, sadness and fear were not the only traits in the character of Manchester workers. There was also a happier side to their personalities. It was expressed well in the lore collected by such self-educated Manchester poets as Edwin Waugh (1819-90) and Ben Brierley (1825-96). These writers attained local fame by recording and imitating Lancashire dialect rhymes, originally part of pre-industrial culture, which had been kept alive and elaborated by rural workers after migration to Manchester and surrounding factory towns. As the modern critic, Martha Vicinus (1973) has shown, an important theme in this dialect literature is pastoral nostalgia. Even in the 1880s, when the most likely place for recitation was a city pub or slum dwelling, the poems continued to present glorified portraits of handloom weavers or idealised descriptions of happy villages, revealing an inability to confront the full range of urban experience and a desire for escape similar to that found in Gissing. But the poems also document the persistence in an urban context of those same traits of gentleness, good humour, gaiety and communal loyalty which Samuel Bamford, in *Passages in the Life of a Radical* (1844), had insistently described as elements in working-class behaviour during the Peterloo riot of 1819 (see above, p. 29). The figures in these poems are hardworking, stoic, sharp in matters of money, sturdy, somewhat slow and heavy physically, and rather monotone in speech patterns at least when compared to city workers in many other parts of England. In addition, they are nearly always members of dissenting religious sects, hardly ever Anglicans or Catholics, and this background makes the poetry greatly sensitive to words and music even if less alert to opportunities for visual imagery. In all these respects, of course, the characters remind one of 'Manchester men' of the middle class. But the poems also show a degree of lightness which would have helped Manchester workers to cope with urban predicaments not faced by the middle class. Singing while weaving is a favourite subject. Other urban versions of rural customs, such as clog dancing and community religious processions, also appear. Especially interesting is a critical yet gentle wit not thought of as part of the middle-class personality. In the twentieth century, this humour was to be carried on in the stage routines of Gracie Fields, the popular comedienne who created a persona based on her Lancashire upbringing. Its clearest expression in late Victorian times was probably the running commentary on Manchester life by Ben Brierley, who undercut the pretensions of big city ways by contrasting them to the simpler, more honest ways of rural Lancashire. It was Brierley who proposed that the new town hall be named the 'Heronry' to honour Manchester's respected but intense town clerk, Joseph Heron. Most workers and even many middle-class residents of Manchester quietly appreciated Brierley's point of view.

C. P. Scott and the Manchester Guardian. If one were to seek a symbol capturing all the traits of character of late Victorian Manchester, even, to some extent, those personified by the Irish and by the women's movement, one could hardly do better than to focus upon the *Manchester Guardian.* By 1900, it was not only the city's most important newspaper, but also a complex urban mirror, one might even say, a talisman, which well-read observers utilised whenever they sought clues to Manchester's identity. The origins of the *Guardian* were closely tied to the early years of industrial Manchester. John Edward Taylor (1791-1844), a young Manchester cotton merchant, had been very concerned that the liberal point of view be represented in the reports of Peterloo making their way from Manchester to London. When the correspondent of *The Times,* John Tyas, was temporarily detained by Lancashire authorities, *The Times* reprinted Taylor's account, thereby making it one of the authoritative interpretations throughout the realm. In 1819, as part of the conservative reaction to Peterloo, Taylor was tried at Lancaster assizes on charges of criminally libelling John Greenwood, leader of the Manchester Tories. When Taylor was acquitted, friends urged him to start a newspaper of his own, which he did in 1821, using capital provided by eleven cotton merchants and manufacturers.

In the early years, there was no guarantee the *Guardian* would survive, let alone become a paper of national stature. It began as one of six Manchester papers, all weeklies, since London was the only city then able to support a daily publication. In the first year, press runs averaged 1,000 copies. Like most provincial papers, the *Guardian* survived largely through advertisements for patent medicines assumed to cure venereal disease, and was read chiefly at inns, pubs and coffeehouses, since the cost of seven pence per issue was not attractive to most individual subscribers. Where many other provincial papers failed or were forced to merge, however, the *Guardian* gradually gathered a steady middle-class readership, with subscribers rising to 3,000 by 1828 and climbing steadily thereafter. Success was due to Taylor's careful reporting: the business skill of his chief printer and managing editor, Jeremiah Garnett; and the paper's care in positioning itself on the political spectrum at the point of moderate liberalism, where it could still hold the respect of Tories because of its honesty and prudence, yet express the views of the expanding business class.

The *Guardian* continued in this pattern for the next several decades, not only under Taylor's leadership, which ended with his death in 1844, but also during that of his two sons, John Edward Taylor the younger and Russell Scott Taylor. Because the *Guardian* was a fixture in Manchester, however, the paper also shared in Manchester's rising fortunes: as national awareness of Manchester increased, national awareness of the *Guardian* increased. In 1842, for example, Sir Robert Peel, the prime minister, quoted the *Guardian* in Parliament during the Corn Law debates – the first mention of the paper in that national forum. In the same way, businessmen in all parts of Britain found that they needed to consult the *Guardian* regularly because of its unrivalled coverage of the cotton industry. By 1867, when the Second Reform Bill was passed, the paper also drew increased readership from political figures in London, who knew that extension of the voting franchise necessitated greater attention to the mood of provincial towns and cities.

In 1872 the *Guardian* increased its national influence in yet another way, when it hired a bright young undergraduate then in his second year at Oxford, Charles Prestwych Scott (1846-1932). Scott was the cousin of John Edward Taylor the younger. Faced with growing responsibilities, Taylor offered him the job of editor, partly to ensure control by the family, partly because his instincts told him Scott possessed great potential. It is difficult to think of any intuitive judgement which has ever been more sound. Over the next three decades, C. P. Scott turned the *Guardian* into a paper of truly national stature.

Scott brought in first-class reviewers, such as George Saintsbury and C. E. Montague, who gave readers greater appreciation for novels, poetry, the fine music performed by the Hallé Orchestra and the growing availability of stage productions in the city. He improved the *Guardian's* coverage of foreign affairs, occasionally overshadowing the London papers, as in the *Guardian's* reportage on the Balkans by James Bryce and Arthur Evans, or the detailed explanation of the turbulent conditions in Ireland. He attracted literate, creative staff members, such as W. T. Arnold, Haslam Mills, Spenser Wilkinson, David Paton and others, who worked for the *Guardian* out of loyalty to its standards, even though they could have drawn higher salaries elsewhere. He also gave readers both in and out of Manchester a heightened sense of the city's character and history, thanks to numerous 'local colour' features on such subjects as Lancashire dialect poems and forgotten Manchester characters. Scott himself wrote leading articles which exhibited strong civic consciousness and a mastery of political theory. His writings in favour of Irish emancipation, for example, became an important factor in that wrenching national debate.

By the time of the first world war, Scott was generally considered to be the most influential Liberal outside of government. When he died in 1932, hundreds of thousands of Lancashire residents lined the streets to pay their respects to his funeral procession, and messages of condolence were received from kings and queens, statesmen and fellow journalists throughout the world.

This response was more than a statement about journalism or politics. It was also an acknowledgement that C. P. Scott and the *Guardian* filled a widespread need for urban symbolism. This could be seen both in Scott's personality and in the role the *Guardian* played as a major urban voice in national debate.

Although his career covered three decades of the twentieth century, Scott was always, in many ways, an almost perfect example of the 'Manchester man' of the late nineteenth century.

He never installed a telephone in his office and never developed the habit of using a typewriter, preferring to write his leading articles at a large wooden desk where he kept a full inkwell and a fresh green blotter. He did not like motor cars. Each day, even in ice and snow, he rode a bicycle three miles to work from his suburban villa, 'The Firs', in the Manchester suburb of Fallowfield. His heavy wool suits were cut along late nineteenth-century lines long after those fashions went out of style. His long, full beard and piercing, intense, brown eyes gave him the appearance of a Victorian sage more than a professional newspaperman. Socially, he was reserved. Morally, he was a contrast to some of his close friends, such as David Lloyd George. As a leader, he was steady, hardworking, autocratic, amazingly

33   C P Scott on his bicycle in the 1920's

fair, distant, not likely to offer pay rises without being asked, susceptible to jealousy, and inspiring – the essential Victorian patriarch leading the essential Victorian family firm. Even more appropriately, he was a strict Unitarian. Thus he continued the spiritual heritage, the dissenter's combination of compassionate idealism and self righteousness, which had prompted John Edward Taylor the elder to name his paper the *Guardian.*

Scott's personal traits both defined and blended with the views the *Guardian* expressed on national political issues. No episode better illustrates this pattern than the *Guardian's* opposition to the Boer war (1899–1901), which prompted angry, jingoistic mobs to gather outside the paper's offices, and caused 7,000 of the paper's 48,000 subscribers to desert it. *Guardian* staff at times felt so beleagured that they characterised the paper's offices as the 'City of Refuge'. But they and Scott persisted, in the process fixing the *Guardian* firmly in the national consciousness. Scott's sentiments, and those of most reporters he hired, were generally against imperialist adventurism and in the 'free trade' tradition of Cobden, Bright and the Anti-Corn Law League, even though many other Manchester citizens had become protectionist by the end of the nineteenth century. This 'little Englander' point of view had first shown itself to a broad national audience when Scott's leading articles of the 1880s had defended Irish emancipation. In 1899, abstract reservation became passionate opposition, and Scott placed the *Guardian* in opposition to any continuation of the war. He thus added an important voice to national debate. The major London papers were at that time controlled by financiers with substantial interests in South Africa, so that important information about the conflict was not being provided. Except for the *Guardian,* readers might never have learned the details of Britain's use of concentration camps during the war, and they might never have received detailed commentaries from J. A. Hobson, the distinguished theorist of imperialism, who was sent on a special visit to South Africa with *Guardian* funds. As the twentieth century progressed, there were to be many similar instances in which the *Guardian* played an important role in debate on major public issues. For many observers, at such moments, the *Guardian* and Manchester were one and the same.

Epilogue

History cannot be packed into neat chronological segments. The year 1900, nevertheless, marked an important transition in the development of Manchester. The end of Queen Victoria's reign was just a year away, along with the change in national mood that accompanied Edward VII's accession. Simultaneously, the economic underpinnings of Manchester were rapidly changing. Faced with international competition in the cotton industry, Manchester diversified into engineering and chemical manufacture. Cotton was no longer the dominant force in shaping the city's life and identity. Thereafter, any symbolism which Manchester evoked was less likely to view the whole of the city as unique or as mirroring the rest of society in rarefied form, and more likely to dwell upon Manchester as typical of many important urban centres with a diversified economy. Increasingly, observers even experienced difficulty in distinguishing Manchester from its hinterland. As the number of roads and buildings and people increased and sprawled over the surrounding countryside, 'Manchester' became synonymous in popular usage with 'Lancashire'. By 1934, when J. B. Priestley published *English Journey*, after a tour of the industrial north to analyse the effects of the world-wide depression, Manchester and Lancashire had blended. 'The real city sprawls all over South Lancashire', he wrote. 'It is an Amazonian jungle of blackened bricks.'

Using a term more fashionable today, one might just as easily say that Manchester had been transformed from 'metropolis' into 'megalopolis'.

Twentieth-century Manchester became the city which manufactured the Rolls-Royce motor car, the Macintosh and the

Lancaster bomber; the place where Ferranti began in electrical engineering and Dunlop in rubber manufacture; the city famous in town planning for Wythenshawe; the parliamentary seat for some years of A. J. Balfour and Winston Churchill; the home of Chaim Weizmann, one of the leaders of the Zionist movement and the first president of Israel; the birthplace of Anthony Burgess, the novelist; the residence and university post for some years of A. J. P. Taylor, the historian; the Liberal bastion of C. P. Scott; the home base of such prominent *Guardian* correspondents as Neville Cardus, the commentator on cricket and music, and Alistair Cooke, the British interpreter of America; the place where Sir Ernest Rutherford did part of the work that earned his Nobel prize in physics; the stronghold of the Manchester United football team; and the home of the Royal Exchange Theatre. As part of the region of Lancashire, Manchester was also the place described by Beatrice Webb in *My Apprenticeship;* by Louis Golding in *Magnolia Street* and other novels; by Margaret Penn in *Manchester Fourteen Miles;* and George Orwell in *The Road to Wigan Pier.* Thus, whoever wishes to study twentieth-century Manchester will need to explore a city very different from its predecessor.

Whether one's interest is in the twentieth century or in earlier times, however, the story of Victorian Manchester will be of enduring interest. In the first place, knowledge of Manchester's past is indispensable if one wishes to understand such present-day features of the city as architecture, political loyalties, religious preferences, ethnic makeup, economic organisation, cultural strengths and weaknesses, and attitudes toward other parts of Britain. Many of the ground rules of these aspects of present-day Manchester life were formulated in Victorian times. All who hope to shape Manchester's future must know how these forces still, in large part, control the city's life today.

The story of Victorian Manchester is also important because it makes certain broad aspects of the nation's past more understandable and thereby takes one a step closer to historical truth. When viewed in terms of nineteenth-century Manchester, familiar features of the British and European historical landscapes often seem rather new. For example: The nineteenth century's difficulties in analysing society are more understandable when one recalls the evidence provided by Manchester that,

34   J B Priestley's Manchester 'An Amazonian jungle of blackened bricks'

in the English speaking world at least, 'slums' were barely
defined as a feature of industrial cities until the 1830s, while
the statistical study of industrial cities only became
systematised in that decade. Similarly, Britain's economic history takes on new dimensions when one learns from a study of
Manchester that many of the advocates of 'free trade' were dri-
ven not only by theories about tariffs and wages but by a political
and social ideology which flirted with the prospect of England
becoming a nation of city-states. Benjamin Disraeli becomes an
even more fascinating figure if one asks what role his special
view of Jerusalem, as expressed in *Coningsby* and *Sybil,* played
in the later years of his life, when he inspired millions with his
social programme for the Tory Party and his version of Britain's
imperial role in the world.

The Crystal Palace exhibition in London in 1851 is not quite
as dominant in one's view of mid-Victorian culture if one recalls
other gatherings, such as Manchester's Art Treasurers Exhibition of 1857. The assumption that industrial cities were
lacking in intellectual aspiration is less tenable for anyone
familiar with the symbolism evoked by the first 'public library'
in Britain and the fledgling years of what is today one of the
great universities of the world. The seldom mentioned capacity
of workers and capitalists to unite, if only briefly, is shown by
the civic patriotism at the opening of Manchester's new town
hall. The history of technology takes on new characteristics
when one recalls that great works of engineering, such as the
Manchester Ship Canal, were built to serve emotional as well
as utilitarian needs. The frequent references to 'Manchester
men' and other representatives of urban personality, noticeable
to all readers of nineteenth-century documents, can be
evaluated with added precision if one knows the complex
evolutions that such terms underwent. And the reputation of
Fredrich Engels is both lessened and enhanced when he is seen
in relation to other observers of Manchester, such as James P.
Kay, Alexis de Tocqueville, Michel Chevalier, and John Prince-
Smith, who were his contemporaries. These are merely a few
aspects of the historical record which take on new meaning in
light of Victorian Manchester's experience.

There is also a spiritual importance in the story of Victorian
Manchester. One characteristic that sets men and women apart

from animals is the capacity for civilised group life. The word 'civilisation' is derived from one of the Latin words for 'city', *civitas*. As urban dwellers, we should therefore do all we can to enhance our capacities for creating and improving city life, particularly in our own time when the whole planet is urbanising. And for such awareness we can find important trial-and-error assistance in the rich experience of nineteenth-century Manchester.

In *The Peloponnesian War,* one of the earliest historians, Thucydides, gave a classic statement of the value of historical example as a guide to the present and future: 'The lack of the fabulous may make my work dull. But I shall be satisfied if it be thought useful by those who wish to know the exact character of events now past which, human nature being what it is, will recur in similar or analogous forms' (I,22). Thucydides wrote of war and statesmanship, not of urbanisation in an industrial civilisation. But the anticipatory motive of his work is as appropriate for the latter challenges facing mankind as it is for the former. The things that happened in nineteenth-century Manchester are worth knowing because, in slightly modified form, they will happen again. As in Manchester so in other cities, there have been and will be riots, plagues, environmental blights, economic disasters, misunderstandings by outsiders and petty rivalries; just as there have been and will be instances of courage, astounding creativity, pride, compassion, economic success and delighted hope in the future. If we wish to be as prepared for these things as possible, we should know what they were like in the past.

Nineteenth-century Manchester provides a warning, perhaps, to our own times, that much of urban life remains beyond comprehension, and that harmonious urban life requires not only an accurate understanding of our own era, but a realisation that the errors of past times are all too easily available for re-use. But there is also inspiration to be gained from Manchester's experience. Although faced with an immense challenge – the appearance of the first industrial city in the history of the world – citizens and observers of Manchester achieved important gains. They invented usable methods of social analysis, as in the quantitative studies of the Statistical Society, the medical studies of J. P. Kay, and the socio-economic analyses of Engels and the Anti-Corn Law League. They devised non-logical means of coping with potentially deranging phenomena, as in the works of Carlyle and the novelists. Although pretentious, they subordinated their biases against intellect and culture, and acted upon imaginative, thoughtful visions of the role of art and learning in an urban-industrial environment. And perhaps most importantly, they developed a many-sided vision of urban self-respect that other cities have sought but not always attained. By modern standards, C. P. Scott and his bicycle may seem stiff and comical. And the self-righteousness of Manchester businessmen and religious leaders remains as difficult for the modern observer to accept as it was for Engels. But at the core of such traits is an admirable quality of which Manchester residents were proud, which visitors noted and encouraged, and which lives on in the Manchester of today. When Englishmen responded to the leadership of the Anti-Corn Law League; when Charles Dickens stated that Manchester's new library was part of 'a great free school'; when prominent thinkers respectfully reviewed the proposal for a University of Manchester; when men and women listened with pleasure to the Hallé concerts; when commentators saw the Ship Canal as an epitome of British courage and inventiveness; and when readers looked to the *Guardian* for accuracy, reliability and good sense – they were paying tribute to an ideal of civic and personal dignity that was uniquely Manchester's but universal as well. This ideal was the product of more than a century's collective effort, the result partly of choice and partly of fate. We should recall it today, because most of us are city creatures ourselves, and Manchester's Victorian age can help us to judge the spiritual consequences of our own thoughts and actions.

Select bibliography

Aikin, John, *A Description of the Country from Thirty to Forty Miles Round Manchester*. London, 1795.

Anderson, Michael, *Family Structure in Nineteenth Century Lancashire*. Cambridge, 1971.

Ashton, Thomas S., *Economic and Social Investigations in Manchester (1833-1933)*. London, 1934.

Aspin, Christopher, *Lancashire: the First Industrial Society*. Rossendale, Lancs., 1969.

Aston, Joseph, *A Picture of Manchester*. Manchester, 1816.

Axon, W. E. A., ed., *An Architectural and General Description of the Town Hall, Manchester*. Manchester, 1878.

Ayerst, David, *The Manchester Guardian: Biography of a Newspaper*. Ithaca, N.Y., 1971.

Baines, Edward, *History of the Cotton Manufacture in Great Britain*, London, 1835.

Bamford, Samuel, *The Autobiography of Samuel Bamford, v. 1, Early Days, together with an Account of the Arrest, etc., v. 2, Passages in the Life of a Radical (1844)*. Ed. with introduction by W. H. Chaloner. London, 1967.

Bazley, Thomas, 'Shall Manchester have a University?', *The Nineteenth Century*, II (April 1877), 113-23.

Becker, Julius, *Das Deutsche Manchestertum: Eine Studie zur Geschichte des wirtschaftpolitischen Individualismus*. Karlsruhe, 1907.

Bell, S. Peter, *Victorian Lancashire*. Newton Abbot, 1974.

Boyson, Rhodes, *The Ashworth Cotton Enterprise*. Oxford, 1970.

Brindley, W. H., ed., *The Soul of Manchester*. Manchester, 1929.

Briggs, Asa, *Victorian Cities*. New York, 1965.

Bruton, F. A., *A Short History of Manchester and Salford.* Manchester, 1924.

Burney, E. L., *Mrs. G. Linnaeus Banks.* Manchester, 1969.

Butterworth, James, *A Complete History of the Cotton Trade.* Manchester, 1823.

Caminada, Jerome, *25 Years of Detective Life.* Manchester, 1895.

Cardus, Neville, *Autobiography.* London, 1947.

Chadwick, Edwin, *Report on the Sanitary Condition of the Labouring Population of Great Britain (1842).* Ed. with Introduction by M. W. Flinn. Edinburgh, 1965.

Chadwick, Mrs Ellis H. (Esther Alice Chadwick), *Mrs. Gaskell, Haunts, Homes, and Stories.* London, 1910.

Chandler, George, *Victorian and Edwardian Manchester and Lancashire from Old Photographs.* London, 1974.

Charlton, H. B., *Portrait of a University, 1851-1951.* Manchester, 1952.

Chorley, Katherine, *Manchester Made Them.* London, 1950.

Clarke, P. F., *Lancashire and the New Liberalism.* Cambridge, 1971.

Credland, W. R., *The Manchester Public Free Libraries. A History and Description and Guide to their Contents and Use.* Manchester, 1899.

Creighton, Charles, *A History of Epidemics in Britain.* 2 v. Cambridge, 1891-4.

Daniels, George W., *The Early English Cotton Industry.* Manchester, 1920.

Darcy, Cornelius P., *The Encouragement of the Fine Arts in Lancashire, 1760-1860.* Manchester, 1976.

Dean, F. R., 'Dickens and Manchester', *The Dickensian,* Vol. 34 (1938), 111-18.

Drescher, Seymour, *Tocqueville and England.* Cambridge, Mass., 1964.

Dyos, Harold J., ed., *The Study of Urban History.* New York, 1968.

Encyclopaedia Britannica. Eleventh edition. New York, 1910-11.

Engels, Friedrich, *The Condition of the Working Class in England.* Translated with notes and introduction by W. O. Henderson and W. H. Chaloner. London, 1958.

Farnie, D. A., 'The commercial development of Manchester in the later nineteenth century', *Manchester Review*, Vol. 7 (Spring 1956), 327-37.

——, *The Manchester Ship Canal and the rise of the Port of Manchester, 1894-1975*. Manchester, 1980.

Faucher, Leon, *Manchester in 1844: Its Present Condition and Future Prospects*. London, 1844.

Fiddes, E., *Chapters in the History of Owens College and of Manchester University, 1851-1914*. Manchester, 1937.

Frangopulo, N. J., ed. *Rich Inheritance: A Guide to the History of Manchester*. Manchester, 1962.

Freeman, Edward A., 'Owens College and Mr. Lowe,' *Macmillan's Magazine*, XXXV (March 1877), 407-16.

Gerin, Winifred, *Elizabeth Gaskell. A Biography*. Oxford, 1976.

Grampp, William D., *The Manchester School of Economics*. Stanford, Calif., 1960.

Green, Leslie P., *Provincial Metropolis: The Future of Local Government in South-East Lancashire*. London, 1959.

Grindon, Leopold H., *Manchester Banks and Bankers*. Second edition. Manchester, 1878.

Hammond, John L., *C. P. Scott of the Manchester Guardian*. London, 1934.

Harnetty, Peter, *Imperialism and Free Trade: Lancashire and India in the mid-nineteenth Century*. Vancouver, B.C., 1972.

Harrison, William, *A History of Manchester Railways*. Manchester, 1967.

Henderson, William O., *The Lancashire Cotton Famine, 1861-1865*. Manchester, 1934.

Himmelfarb, Gertrude, *The Idea of Poverty. England in the Early Industrial Age*. New York, 1984.

Hindle, G. B., *Provision for the Relief of the Poor in Manchester, 1754-1826*. Manchester, 1975.

Hobson, John A., *Richard Cobden. The International Man* (1919). New edition with introduction by Neville Masterman. London, 1968.

Holt, Elizabeth Gilmore, *The Art of All Nations: 1850-1873*. New York, 1981.

Hughes, Thomas, *James Fraser, Second Bishop of Manchester. A Memoir, 1818-1885*. London, 1889.

Hurt, John, *Education in Evolution*. London, 1971.

Jacobs, Jane, *The Economy of Cities*. New York, 1969.

Jenkins, F., 'The making of a municipal palace: Manchester Town Hall,' *Country Life*, CXLI (16 February 1967), 336-9.

Kargon, Robert, *Science in Victorian Manchester: Enterprise and Expertise*. Manchester, 1977.

Kay, James P., *The Moral and Physical Condition of the Working Classes Employed in the Cotton Manufacture of Manchester*. London, 1832.

Kay-Shuttleworth, Sir James (James P. Kay), *Four Periods of Public Education*. London, 1862.

Kellett, John R., *The Impact of Railways on Victorian Cities*. London, 1969.

Kennedy, Michael, *The Hallé Tradition*. Manchester, 1960.

Lansbury, Coral, *Elizabeth Gaskell: The Novel of Social Crisis*. New York, 1975.

Leech, Sir Bosdin, *History of the Manchester Ship Canal*. 2 v. Manchester, 1907.

Longmate, Norman, *The Hungry Mills*. London, 1978.

Machray, Robert, 'Gates and Pillars of the Empire. No. IV. Manchester and Salford Illustrated'. *Pearson's Magazine*, II (July 1896), 3-17.

Makepeace, Chris, *Manchester as it Was*. 6 v. Manchester, 1972-7.

Maltby, Samuel E., *Manchester and the Movement for National Elementary Education, 1800-1870*. Manchester, 1918.

Marshall, Leon S., *The Development of Public Opinion in Manchester, 1780-1820*. Syracuse, N.Y., 1946.

McLachlan, Herbert, 'Cross Street Chapel in the life of Manchester,' *Memoirs and Proceedings of the Manchester Literary and Philosophical Society*, Vol. 84 (1939-41), 29-41.

McCord, Norman, *The Anti-Corn Law League, 1838-1846*. London, 1958.

Midwinter, Eric, *Law and Order in Early Victorian Lancashire*. York, 1968.

——, *Social Administration in Lancashire, 1830-1860*. Manchester, 1969.

Mills, William Haslam, *The Manchester Guardian: A Century of History*. London, 1921.

Millward, Roy, *Lancashire: An Illustrated Essay on the History of the Landscape*. London, 1955.

Morley, John, *The Life of Richard Cobden*. 2 v. London, 1881.

Morris, R. J., *Cholera 1832*. London, 1976.

Mosse, George L., 'The Anti-League: 1844-1846', *Economic History Review*. Vol. 17, Nos. 1 and 2 (1947-8), 134-42.

Munford, Arthur, *William Ewart, M.P., 1798-1869: Portrait of A Radical*. London, 1960.

Newland, F. W., 'The City of Manchester', *Sunday at Home*, XXI (January 1900), 149-51; (February), 226-32; (March), 321-5; (April), 370-5.

[North, Christopher], 'Manchester poetry', *Blackwood's Edinburgh Magazine*, IX (April 1821), 196-202.

Owen, David, *The Manchester Ship Canal*. Manchester, 1983.

Pardon, G. F., *The Manchester Conductor; A Guide for Visitors to the Great Art Treasures Exhibition*. Manchester, 1857.

Paton, David, 'The Manchester Ship Canal', *Good Words*, XXXIII (February 1892), 100-7.

Porritt, Edward, 'Manchester Ship Canal', *Yale Review*, III (November 1894), 296-310.

Prentice, Archibald, *Historical Sketches and Personal Recollections of Manchester* (1851). New edition with introduction by Donald Read. London, 1970.

——, *The History of the Anti-Corn Law League*. 2 v. London, 1853.

Priestley, J. B., *English Journey*. London, 1934.

Raumer, Friedrich von, *England in 1835*. Tr. Sarah Austin and H. E. Lloyd. Philadelphia, 1836.

Read, Donald, *The English Provinces, c. 1760-1960; a study in influence*. London, 1964.

——, *Peterloo: The 'Massacre' and its Background*. Manchester, 1958.

——, *Press and People, 1790-1850; Opinion in Three English Cities*. London, 1961.

Redford, Arthur, *The History of Local Government in Manchester*. 3 v. London, 1939-40.

——, *Labour Migration in England, 1800-1850*. Second edition, revised and edited by W. H. Chaloner. Manchester, 1964.

——, *Manchester Merchants and Foreign Trade*. 2 v. Manchester, 1934 and 1956.

Roberts, Jacqueline, *Working Class Housing in Nineteenth Century Manchester*. Manchester, 1975.

Roberts, Robert, *The Classic Slum*. Manchester, 1971.
———, *A Ragged Schooling*. Manchester, 1976.
Rodgers, H. B., 'The suburban growth of Victorian Manchester', *Transactions of the Manchester Geographical Society* (1961-2), 1-12.
Ryan, Rachael, *A Biography of Manchester*. London, 1937.
Saintsbury, George, *Manchester*. London, 1887.
Sanderson, Michael, *The Universities and British Industry, 1850-1970*. London, 1972.
Silver, Arthur W., *Manchester Men and Indian Cotton, 1847-1872*. Manchester, 1966.
Simon, E. D., *A City Council from Within*. London, 1926.
Simon, Sheena D., *A Century of City Government; Manchester, 1838-1938*. London, 1938.
Smelser, Neil J., *Social Change in the Industrial Revolution. An Application of Theory to the British Cotton Industry*. Chicago, 1959.
Smith, Frank, *The Life and Work of Sir J. Kay-Shuttleworth*. London, 1923.
Smith, Goldwin, 'University extension', *Fortnightly Review*, XXIX (January 1878), 85-95.
Smith, Sheila M., *The Other Nation: The Poor in English Novels of the 1840's and 1850's*. Oxford, 1980.
Spiers, G. Robert, 'The Victorian city and the frightened poets', *Victorian Studies*, XI, supplement (Summer 1968), 627-40.
Stange, G. Robert, 'The Victorian city and the frightened poets', *Victorian Studies*, XI, supplement (Summer 1968), 627-40.
Stewart, Cecil, *The Stones of Manchester*. London, 1956.
Taylor, A. J. P., 'The world's great cities (1) Manchester', *Encounter*. Vol. 42 (March 1957), 3-13.
[Taylor, Issac], 'Education for the metropolis of manufactures', *North British Review*, XVIV (November 1855), 1-49.
Taylor, William Cooke, *Notes of a Tour in the Manufacturing Districts of Lancashire*. Second edition. London, 1842.
Tillotson, Kathleen, *Novels of the 1840's*. Oxford, 1954.
Tocqueville, Alexis de, *Journeys to England and Ireland*. Translated by G. Lawrence and K. P. Mayer. Edited by J. P. Mayer. London, 1958.
Ure, Andrew, *The Cotton Manufacture of Great Britain*. 2 v. London, 1861.

Vicinus, Martha, 'Literary voices of an industrial town. Manchester, 1810-1870', in H. J. Dyos and Michael Wolff, eds, *The Victorian City*. 2 v. London, 1973. II, 739-61.

Vigier, François, *Change and Apathy: Liverpool and Manchester during the Industrial Revolution*. Cambridge, Mass., 1970.

Walmsley, Robert, *Peterloo: The Case Re-Opened*. Manchester, 1969.

Webb, Beatrice (née Potter), *My Apprenticeship*. London, 1966.

Wheeler, James, *Manchester, its Political, Social, and Commercial History, Ancient and Modern*. London, 1836.

Wilson, Edmund, *To the Finland Station*. New York, 1953.

Wood, Kinder, *A Prospect of Manchester and its Neighbourhood*. Manchester, 1813.

Young, G. M., *Victorian England: Portrait of an Age* Oxford, 1936; Second edition, New York, 1964.

Index